Life Is But A Breath

An amazing story of fight for survival against all odds!

Agnès Sanders

Agnès Sanders
Life is But a Breath
An amazing story of fight for survival against all odds!
1st edition

ISBN: 0-9723406-0-2

French edition:
Agnès Sanders, *La vie est un souffle*. Le long combat d'une mère contre la maladie de son enfant. Mazerolles, France, Empreinte temps présent, 1992 – Collection Sources.
German edition:
Agnès Sanders, *Ein Hauch von Hoffnung*. Anne soll leben – Eine Mutter kämpft für ihr Kind. Moers, Germany, Brendow Buch Kunst Verlag, 2000. Aus dem Französischen von Andrea Erdmann.

Published by:

Enable! Media [1]
16076 NW Joscelyn St.
Beaverton, OR 97006

www.enable-media.org

To contact publisher: publishing@enable-media.org

Cover design by Rachel Aw

[1] Produced for *Enable! Media* by Technidata Publishers.

To all the children of the Hayy Al Gharbeh shantytown who are helpless when sickness strikes. To Sa'er, a happy little boy who died at three; to Sara who remained blind; to Najwa who will never walk.

But also to Hassan who is overcoming heart disease, to Kamar and Maha who can see again, to Omar fighting sickle cell anemia. To all children whose parents cannot afford to pay for health care.

Life in this world is not fair, but:

"When the perishable has been clothed with the imperishable, and the mortal with immortality, then the saying that is written will come true: 'Death has been swallowed up in victory'" (I Corinthians 15:53-54, NIV)

Foreword

Had we known on that day in August, 1981 what trials and challenges were to come in the next few months and years, we might have been paralyzed by fear. But, at this point, we were mercifully spared from knowing the details of days to come, and we were able to rejoice in the birth or our second child, Anne. Life went on as we adjusted to a new member in the family. But this all came to a sudden end in December as our family faced a crisis that we could not have envisioned in our most vivid imaginings. Through it all, we learned the true meaning of God's love and care for us. Many thoughts were impressed upon us over the coming years, but they can all be summed up by:

> "...My grace is sufficient for you, for my power is made perfect in weakness..." [1]

This book recounts a chapter in the life of our family: Ten years (1981-1991) deeply affected by the life-threatening illness of our daughter, but also shaped by trust in a Divine Creator.

This is a true story. We lived through these events as a family and have described them here, to the best of our recollection, exactly as they took place. Most of the names of hospitals and individuals, with the exception of those of family and friends, have been changed to ensure confidentiality.

Special thanks for the realization of this English language edition go to Ms. Mary Hill for her competent and diligent general proofreading and to Dr. Ruth Bennie for her skills in reviewing the English medical vocabulary and meticulous stylistic proofreading. To Julie Hannouche who helped launch this project by proofreading the first two chapters. A very special and affectionate thank you to my son Matthieu for the

---

[1] II Corinthians 12:9.

translation from French and to my husband Paul for the word processing, general editing and numerous hours invested in our common project. Much gratitude as well to A. Dale Aufrecht of Enable! Media for his encouragement, counsel and professional help, indispensable for the realization of this book.

Agnès Sanders

Chapter 1

Like a Vapor

Our life toppled over on December 4th, 1981. We had gone through a few jolts since mid-November of that year, yet we believed they were part of life's usual worries and concerns and we kept our composure.

On the 4th of December, the ground shook. For the first time, we became clearly aware that death was near, ready to take our baby away from us. All other aspects of our lives suddenly became insignificant.

Our little Anne was just three months old. Before having children, I had believed losing an infant must not be such a catastrophe. How wrong I was! From the first week of Anne's life, we grew attached to this small, ungrateful being with a love that surpassed logical reasoning.

Suddenly, it became impossible to make any plans. The future was uncertain:

> *"Now listen, you who say, 'Today or tomorrow we will go to this or that city, spend a year there, carry on business and make money.' Why, you do not even know what will happen tomorrow. What is your life? You are a mist that appears for a little while and then vanishes."* [1, 2]

Until now, my husband Paul and I were goal-oriented achievers, not motivated by money, as the man portrayed in the above passage, but rather by personal achievement, a more subtle form of pride than the quest for fortune.

---

[1] All biblical quotations, unless otherwise noted, are taken from the New International Version.

[2] James 4:13-14.

Ten years before, in 1970, I had made the most important decision of my life. After a few months of reflection, I had accepted the existence and rule of the Divine Creator and had decided to follow His will for my life. I knew instinctively that this change in direction, or "conversion," was going to transform my life entirely.

We were devout Christians. We considered ourselves happy, yet we disregarded certain essential values. We had much to discover about the true riches God had in store for us. Until now I had undergone no humiliating failure, great disappointment, or immense grief. I had felt a certain pride in this, as if I should receive the credit. Deep down, I thought that I was doing quite a good job and that others, after all, only had to work hard if they wanted to succeed.

Birth

Anne was born on August 25, 1981. Now, in France, because of vacation patterns, nothing serious takes place during the month of August! I was in fact expected to deliver on September 12, but babies do not know they shouldn't disturb their parents in August. Anne, therefore, arrived 19 days ahead of her due date in a small suburban Paris clinic where one floor was closed for want of available personnel and probably, for want of expectant mothers, who had gone on holiday and were patiently awaiting September to deliver.

The clinic called the substitute obstetrician (mine had also gone on holiday), who happened to be in Paris in August as his wife was about to give birth. We actually delivered on the same day, making the obstetrician a bit nervous and hurried but also delighted that my labor went so quickly and easily. I saw this man for only about ten minutes of my life. I believe he never knew of the dramatic events that occurred in Anne's life. Even if he had heard about these events, it would probably not have troubled him. Life functions in such a way that events which devastate us affect others very little. It is probably better this way, but a balance between compassion and competency is often difficult to find. The medical profession is no exception.

Anne was apparently doing well. She weighed about 2.9 kilograms (six pounds), a reasonable weight for a slightly premature child. She was *cyanotic*, that is her hands, feet and the area around her mouth were a purplish color. I tried to shrug off my worries by thinking of all the purple babies I had seen emerge from their mother's wombs during my obstetrics internship. Each time I was certain these babies were dead, but after a few seemingly unending seconds they cried and took on a beautiful pink color.

I was nevertheless worried about this persistent *cyanosis* and spoke to a pediatric assistant about the problem. She told me the pediatrician was on holiday. We could contact the doctor on call but only in case of an emergency. Since I was a physician myself, however, she would bring me a stethoscope so I could examine my baby. I do not recall for sure whether I eventually used the stethoscope or not. I believe I did, but this did not reassure me.

It struck me that when it was convenient for the medical staff to view me as a doctor, I was asked to lay aside my role as mother. However, at other times, for example, when they were feeling unsure of themselves, my presence made them uneasy. At such times they tended to relegate me to my role as mother and ask me to leave the examination room. I do not blame them. I am also part of the medical community and can identify with them. In any working situation some people are likeable while others are less so. Some are tired, uptight, brave, lazy or proud, and some have simply had a bad day following a sleepless night on call.

Five Weeks of Family Life

Six days after Anne's birth, we left the maternity ward. She weighed six pounds and did not seem in a hurry to regain her birth weight. I nevertheless preferred to leave this place where medical assistance seemed almost nonexistent. Since Anne's *cyanosis* was not as apparent as before, I decided to leave and informed the resident of my decision. He had no objection.

Before leaving the ward, Anne underwent a mandatory pediatric examination, whose results were to be recorded in her health booklet – the child's medical record kept by the parents. I was looking forward to finally seeing a pediatrician, but I was disappointed. Hasty, grumpy and monosyllabic, he determined in five minutes' time that Anne was normal. His examination was less than thorough. I believe he never learned of what transpired later.

Although this pediatrician was neither friendly nor thorough, it turned out to be a blessing for us, for we thus gained five happy weeks, blissfully ignoring Anne's problems. A more conscientious pediatrician would have performed a more serious examination, taken my worries into account and probably noticed something abnormal while listening to Anne's chest. Had he requested an X-ray, he would have been astounded by the results and Anne would have begun her tour of hospitals five weeks earlier with no additional benefit.

The arrival of a newborn child is always a great joy. We were exhilarated to finally have our daughter with us, but at the same time felt a tremendous responsibility.

We enjoyed five peaceful weeks as a family. We inwardly took credit for having previously given life to a handsome little boy and now Anne, a pretty little girl. The congratulations of many friends, though motivated by good intentions, implied that our good fortune was all our doing. These congratulations implied that those who could not perform such feats really possessed no talent at all!

The First Serious Worries

Anne was now one month old. She was doing well with slow but steady weight gain. I decided to take her for a pediatric consultation to a suburban hospital I knew, having worked there as a medical student a few years before.

The main reason for the consultation was a tenacious rash Anne had contracted which defied all my attempts to treat it. I was pleased to be more serene with Anne than I had been with my first child, Matthieu. I was now determined to look at the bright side of everything, and not worry unnecessarily about Anne as I had about him.

During the routine examination, the pediatrician discovered a heart murmur. He advised me to come back with Anne five days later for a pediatric cardiology consultation. In spite of my positive resolutions, I felt anxiety beginning to grow. I repeatedly tried to convince myself that heart murmurs are not uncommon and usually benign among infants. As soon as I arrived home, however, I grabbed my stethoscope and listened to her myself. I was troubled by the intensity of the murmur that I heard. I used my stethoscope several times that day, then decided not to touch it anymore in order to avoid constantly feeding my anxiety. This was difficult. Her post-natal *cyanosis* immediately came to my mind, as I began to imagine all the potential cardiac malformations. Could this account for her difficulty in gaining weight? Did she not still show signs of *cyanosis* around her mouth? How I yearned to be reassured immediately! The day following the examination, however, was a Sunday, and no ordinary Sunday at that.

True Values

Sunday, October 4, 1981, was the date we had chosen to dedicate our newborn child to God before our church, friends and family. Our trust in the Creator was about to be seriously challenged. Indeed, what is faith but trust in Him who created us? And what does this faith amount to, if our trust fades away in the face of adversity? If my son Matthieu fell and hurt himself, he cried and came to me. Did he lose his trust in me because he had fallen? Did he question my love because he had hurt himself? No, his trust was enough to reassure him. But how weak our faith can be!

It was a particularly moving ceremony. On that day, we celebrated Anne's birth and dedication, and the 80th birthday of her great-grandmother. We were also saying goodbye to our church, which we were leaving to help begin another church several miles away.

The entire family had gathered for a weekend of celebration. We felt that this was a turning point in our lives. It was, but not in the way we had planned. It seemed to us the future had become clear after several years of uncertainty. We had spent five years without having children, fearing that we would never be able to have any, but now we had two. We had encountered difficulties in finding a place to live, but now were moving into a nice house. I had completed my medical studies and was satisfied with my part-time job working in preventive medicine. Paul was working on a doctorate in history and, being a pastor as well, was preparing for his church-planting ministry.

In a sense, therefore, it was our entire future that we were dedicating to God that day along with our new child. A medical student, who was a close friend of ours, had written a song for the occasion and sang it to those present. We then publicly testified to our trust in God and to our personal commitment in raising Anne as wise managers of her physical, psychological and spiritual life. At that moment, we did not share our recent fears for her health with others, but those few sentences by which we dedicated her entirely to God left an even more profound impression in my heart because of the events of the preceding day. This prepared me for the storm that was to come in the following days.

We had entrusted our child to God and knew that her life was in His hands. It was not easy, as we would later see, to relinquish the right to see our daughter live. It is normal to want to keep the child you love with you, and God understands our fears. We should not feel guilty about these feelings, though we should not allow them to dominate us. Devout Christians, in particular, sometimes feel guilty about feelings of anxiety and sadness.

Because of varying temperaments, some of us succumb to the chronic temptation of false guilt more often than others. God knows us, and He is there to free us from this tenacious feeling of anxiety. He allows us to be tested by anxiety ("tempted" and "tested" are both translations of the same Greek word in the New Testament), but this testing should not bring guilt unless we allow it to be a chronic state. It took me years to realize this truth, and I am still learning how to integrate it into my life.

When we dedicated Anne to God on that 4th day of October, we had no reason to think her life would hinge on a narrowed trachea, one millimeter in diameter. For us, although we did not immediately realize it, it was the beginning of an immense adventure during which we learned that this life holds few guarantees.

It was, indeed, just when everything seemed to be going well that everything crumbled around us; our new house, our professional situation, everything that had seemed so important to us suddenly lost its significance. Nothing mattered but the life or death of our child. As we faced this, we had no choice, no way of avoiding being confronted with our true values. I can establish a parallel with a choice that we all must eventually face in our existence: spiritual life or death. How futile and insignificant everything else in life should seem to us in light of this choice!

Although we do not understand all of the reasons for suffering, we find at least that it brings us back to basic values. We lose the pride that made us feel self-sufficient, and our shield of rebellion against God, sometimes disguised as indifference, begins to vanish. Paul and I had unwittingly become focused on secondary values of success. Thankfully we had previously opened our eyes to life's essential issues and had not overlooked the discovery of God.

First Contact With the Hospital

The 8th of October finally arrived. I felt a sense of haste mixed with apprehension. My need to know, however, was stronger than my fear, and my fundamental optimism made me impatient to see this examination at the hospital take place.

Along with my impatience, I had the discomforting impression that Anne was entering the world of hospital patients who indeed must "patiently" wait for long periods of time and who, because of an undefined rule, are not considered quite as responsible as other individuals. It is as if being pregnant or having a sick child took away part of your reasoning capacities, part of your responsibility. I still clearly remember those prenatal checkups during which I was asked in a paternalistic tone to "go potty." Why are patients treated like children? I have often noticed that the least qualified members of hospital personnel are those who most commonly act in such a way. Perhaps this is a way for them to withstand the uneasy hierarchy existing in hospitals; a way to find, in the patients, people weaker than themselves. As for physicians, although apparently cold and unsympathetic, they do not usually treat patients as children though they sometimes ignore them, which is another form of disrespect.

When I arrived with Anne, she was doing very well. We had only come to the hospital because of a mere heart murmur. I was therefore looking forward to a diagnosis confirming a benign condition, thus allowing her to enter the world of normal people once again.

Before seeing the pediatrician and the cardiologist, a chest X-ray and an EKG were performed. We went first to the X-ray department. I had worked there as a medical student and was immediately well received.

After the traditional moment of fondness toward the former student's new baby, I was led to the X-ray room. Until that moment, Anne had never gone through uncomfortable examinations, and for the first time, I became aware of the injustice of making a child go through an ordeal she does not understand.

Even for a child as young as Anne, it would probably have been possible to make the procedure more bearable. The staff could have talked to her gently, undressed her calmly and slowly, and laid her softly on the X-ray table. Instead she was suspended by a hook connected to the wrists with canvas bracelets. Her unsupported head hung limply. Her feet were placed in holes in a plank that was supposed to support her bottom. The plank was actually too low with respect to the hook and did not support her at all. I could see my poor baby pathetically hanging by the wrists, naked, screaming from terror, cold and perhaps pain.

This resembled a torture scene and I had a moment of revulsion as well as an overwhelming urge to take my baby with me, away from those who almost appeared to me as child abusers. They did not suspect my anger and were doing their job rather seriously on the whole, while making small talk about unrelated things with, of course, no intention of harming Anne.

I understood why parents are usually asked not to enter the examining room under the pretext of safety or protection of the parents. It is easier for medical staff to work on an object rather than another human being. Patients are consequently more or less dehumanized and turned into objects on which one can work calmly. If the patients' loved ones are there, a personal relationship is established which protects the patient from being dehumanized. The medical staff is then less at ease.

My desire to leave the hospital with my daughter in my arms was short-lived. I knew I had to submit and remain there, as I was unable to change the conditions of the examination. The most effective method in such a situation goes against our instincts; in this case, it is preferable to be as amiable as possible with the personnel, which results in more kindness toward our child.

The first X-rays were not satisfactory, and Anne had to remain in this terribly uncomfortable position as we waited for a second round of films to be developed and examined. I stayed close to her, caressing her head and trying to comfort her in that awful position, which of course was impossible.

These long minutes led me to think of my own relationship with God. We often find ourselves, as Anne did, in a painful situation that makes no sense to us. Yet our Father, who created us and knows everything about us, knows why we are going through such pain. He assures us of His love throughout our trials even when the situation makes no sense to us. He does not try to make us understand why things happen when we cannot understand them. Instead he promises us that we can trust Him and rest in Him because:

> "...*we know that in all things God works for the good of those who love Him.*" [3]

The Shock

In the hallway of the X-ray department, I was given an envelope containing the films for the cardiologist. I was not expecting anything in particular from the X-rays, thinking the EKG and the stethoscope examination would explain the origin of the heart murmur much better. Without thinking, I took the film out of the envelope to take a look at it, using the light coming through the window near the staircase. I was shocked. Though the left half of the chest was dark, like a normal pulmonary image, the right half of the chest was completely white, as if there were no air on that side. I did not, in my confusion, even notice that there was no shadow cast by the heart. I did not understand. This seemed completely unrelated to the heart problem for which I had come. I immediately thought of a technical X-ray error.

I pulled out the written report enclosed with the X-ray. The first thing I saw were the words "CLINICAL DETAILS PLEASE," underlined three times, followed by the following typed words: "total opacity of the right hemithorax." I can understand the frustration of the radiologist who tried to interpret Anne's X-ray without any information from the clinical examination. Indeed, a patient with an X-ray showing half his chest as totally opaque must be suffering from something serious. Why then, hadn't the hospital given appropriate clinical information to the radiologist?

It was incomprehensible. My baby was doing very well and had neither pleurisy nor pneumonia. The X-rays must be totally in error! Still, fear overwhelmed me. Why had they redone the films so many

---

[3] Romans 8:28.

times? My anxiety was mounting, as was my disbelief. I had come to be reassured and now everything seemed to be getting more complicated!

I felt like running to see the cardiologist, brandishing the X-ray before his eyes, asking for an explanation, and hearing him suggest a reassuring hypothesis. Instead, I waited like everyone else in the waiting room, feeling my stomach aching with anxiety and my heart pounding, while I lovingly looked at my baby, sleeping calmly in my arms, fortunately unaware of my inner agitation.

I talked to God, but only in short sentences, incapable of elaborating complex thoughts: "What is going on, Lord? What is going on? Protect Anne, Lord. She's yours. Take care of her." My thoughts went back to the incomprehensible X-ray picture. What would the cardiologist have to say about that?

We were finally called, and the examination began in a most ordinary way. I was not going to go in, holding the X-ray, while exclaiming, "Look at this complete opacity on the right side!" They had to make the discovery themselves. I handed the envelope to the cardiologist as if it were a package of explosives. She did not, however, seem interested at all and laid the envelope on the desk... and nothing had yet exploded. The pediatrician handed the infant to the cardiologist, a somewhat elderly, sweet-looking lady. "Here is a five-week old baby who has no clinical trouble, in whom I discovered a heart murmur by chance. I'd like you to tell me what you think. Her mom is one of my former medical students," he said.

During that time, two assistants had undertaken the task of conducting the EKG. Anne, once again, was naked and awake, and the assistants, in order to keep her from screaming, had given her wet gauze to suck on, which Anne did not really appreciate. The cardiologist waited to have the EKG, which she looked at rapidly before saying almost immediately: "You must have made a mistake. The leads are reversed." The two nurses looked at each other, surprised, not particularly desiring to redo a difficult examination on a screaming and kicking baby.

Yielding to the authority of the cardiologist, they began their work once again while mumbling that they did not see how the leads could possibly have been reversed.

As for me, I did not make the connection between this exchange and the strange X-ray I had just seen. While waiting for the assistants to perform the second EKG, the cardiologist finally took the pictures and hung them on the X-ray viewing screen behind the desk.

I held my breath. The two doctors observed the pictures for a few seconds without saying anything. The pressure mounted within me. After what seemed like an eternity, the woman turned around and told the two nurses: "Don't start over, the leads were not reversed. This is a case of *dextrocardia*."

I repeated the word to myself: "dextrocardia." Her heart was on the right side! Heart on the right side? Thoughts flooded my mind: having your heart on the right side is an oddity, not a disease. One can live perfectly well with a heart on the right side.

During that time, the cardiologist was studying the X-rays and the EKG: "There is no '*situs inversus*,' [4] she said, only an inverted position of the heart. The location or even the existence of the right lung, however, needs to be verified, because it is not visible. It could be hidden behind the heart and the thymus," she said.

She was not really talking to me so much as trying to make sense out of a most unusual situation in order to make a diagnosis. She was talking to herself and including the pediatrician and me in her thoughts. I was at least given the right to participate in the discovery, which is not always the case. Physicians often try to spare the parents at critical moments by making them physically leave the room or by using a medical jargon that is incomprehensible to them. If I had not been part of the medical corps, I would have understood little. Would that have been better or worse? I prefer to understand

---

4   Situs inversus – reversal of all organs from their normal side to the opposite one.

what is happening, even at the cost of greater anxiety, for anxiety is the result of unexplained fear of the unknown.

The cardiologist finally sat down and talked to me in an effort to reassure me, as she would have any other mother: "Dextrocardia is not a serious condition in itself. It is extremely rare, but not serious. We do however have to make sure that there are no cardiac or vascular malformations, and especially, explain the presence of that murmur. I think it would be best to perform an echocardiogram at the University Hospital Center," she said.

I remained silent, too flabbergasted to say anything. What could I say? This was the way things were, and no discussion could change that. I had not yet begun to ask questions about details as I was still trying to make sense of it all. Feeling at once powerless, yet strangely serene, I sensed just as clearly the awesome power of Anne's Creator. "This is incomprehensible to us," I thought, "but God knows exactly what is happening."

To break the silence, the doctor said in a soft voice: "I know how you must feel and I understand your concern. I am going to try to set an appointment for an echocardiogram immediately so that you don't have to wait, because there is usually a three-week waiting period. I know that if she were my child, I would want to know right away."

Several thoughts crossed my mind. First of all, I imagined the cardiologist with her own children. Was she married? Did she even have children? Could she really understand? I was thankful to her for speaking to me in a personal manner, for involving herself in the situation and talking about children she may not even have had. Either way, she was talking to a woman, putting herself on my level, and for that reason, I felt very positive about her.

Her simple words: "If she were my child," had touched me profoundly, although I could not say why. It was probably because she had left her role as a doctor for a few minutes to speak as a woman to another woman's heart. I had only nodded and said I indeed did not want to have to live for three weeks with the uncertainty of a severe malformation. A benign murmur was now out of the question. The unlikely was becoming likely, and the worst was now possible.

I was also grateful for the fact that she was going to take care of scheduling the appointment at the University Hospital Center herself. There is nothing more discouraging, when you are worried about the health of a loved one, than trying to reach a hospital service by telephone. The switchboard operator often connects you to the wrong department. When you finally are connected to the right department, you often wait on hold until the line unexplainably disconnects.

If a doctor calls, it simplifies the process. Once the initial switchboard hurdles are overcome, it is often easier to reach someone in charge. For this reason, I sometimes had to call as "Anne Sanders' treating physician" in order to obtain information from a doctor.

The cardiologist obtained an appointment for October 12, four days later, because she had called herself and made a point of saying "the mom is a doctor." I did not like this favoritism, but was thankful for it at the same time. How often individual interest finds itself in conflict with noble ideals! Yet if everything worked well for everybody, favoritism would be unnecessary.

It is probably true that a mother who is also a doctor needs quicker and more precise answers to her questions than another mother who would tend to rely more on the expertise of renowned medical professionals. I, too, had much confidence in the best specialists, but I know their limits. I know that medicine is far from an exact science and that we should not resist admitting there are things we do not know. We should rather accept our limitations while striving to better understand.

Chapter 2
The Spiral of Fear

Visit in Cardiology

On October 12th, I brought Anne, now seven weeks old, to the regional University Hospital Center. The feeling we had become locked into "the medical machine" was becoming increasingly real. I paced the large hallways of the hospital, carrying my bassinet with one arm and the required file of documents with the other. First challenge: get beyond the cash registers. There, the typical greeting was: "sit down and wait," without a smile nor a "hello." I began to think we were greeted more cordially at the bank! (A matter of money, perhaps?)

Second challenge: finding an elevator. You need to find the right one and hope it will work. The first elevator we found was reserved for stretchers, the second one for patients, the third one stopped only at odd-numbered floors, while I needed to go to the eighth floor. I finally found the elevator, which stopped at even-numbered floors and was not reserved for medical personnel. I pressed the call button. Then I waited. A small group of people joined me to wait for the elevator. Some gave Anne tender smiles. This human warmth expressed in such cold surroundings gave me comfort.

After a few minutes, some simply gave up and took the stairway. How could I climb to the eighth floor carrying my bassinet? At long last, the elevator arrived, releasing a full load of white-gowned staff, mixed with visitors.

Eighth floor: the Infantile Cardiology Unit. There I discovered a completely different world; everyone was friendly, welcoming. A nurse led us to the ultrasound room and gave Anne a pacifier, which she appreciated more than wet gauze. It does not take much to satisfy a seven-week old baby, but it does take sensitivity. Anne needed to be very calm for the examination to proceed.

All around me, doctors were commenting on various medical records. The terms of diagnosis mentioned were impressive, representing serious malformations of which I only had a few academic notions. For them, however, this was simply routine. I felt that my daughter's destiny was going to be revealed to me in the next few minutes. The examination began. I saw Anne's heart beating on the screen, rapid and delicate. The small cardiac valves, thin as sheets of paper, were animated by harmonious movement, examples of this wonderful human machine that beats millions of times without failing. Other doctors approached us, interested in this new, unusual case. The examiner gave a running commentary to his colleagues: the cardiac cavities are normal, the pulmonary artery as well, there is no defect in the septua, the aorta is in place, the heart is simply "dextro-rotated." The examining doctor then turned to Dr. Mera, the friendly lady who had scheduled my appointment. He looked surprised, even a little disappointed: "There is nothing wrong with this child." She almost apologized: "Yes, well, she does have the heart on the right side... I thought there might be some malformations..."

I was all smiles! Good news at last! I was glad he was disappointed! As for Dr. Mera, she seemed sincerely relieved. This made me appreciate her even more. The life of a child was more important to her than a "good" diagnosis. She took me aside, saying: "Come into my office; we can do an EKG, if you'd like." She stopped for a moment, looked at me, and asked for my permission: "Is it all right if we do an EKG again?" Of course it was all right! I did appreciate the fact, nevertheless, that she consulted me, that she did not consider my daughter a laboratory animal.

A few minutes later, a short man joined us. He was kind. but reserved. I first thought that he was a resident, until Dr. Mera introduced him to me as Professor Sapiero, chief of the cardiology department. Apologizing for the nuisance of the examinations, he accompanied us as we went for the EKG, as well as for a more thorough clinical examination.

After the examination, Dr. Mera turned to me and addressed me in a reassuring tone: "Everything seems to confirm that this heart is normal, except for its position on the right and the murmur, which could be due to a persistence of the *ductus arteriosis*." [1] She explained: "We need to confirm the opening of the patient's ductus arteriosis and its flow as well as run more tests to ascertain the consequences on pulmonary pressures, but we're not in a hurry. If she continues to tolerate this condition well, we will postpone closure for a few months, at least until she's gained a little weight."

Feeling reassured, I found the ability to speak again and asked for more details:

"How will I know if she is tolerating this anomaly?"

"You'll see if she is short of breath as you breast-feed her, if she becomes tired quickly, or if she sweats a lot," Dr. Mera answered.

"Will I really notice this?" I asked, "Anne often stops during feeding-time. Is it because she is out of breath?"

"No, you will know, they tell me, if this is the case. It will be obvious, no need for unnecessary worry," Dr. Mera replied

I then dared to ask the question that had me preoccupied, asking as coolly as I could, despite my immense dread:

"Isn't there a risk of sudden infant death?" He seemed to hesitate for a moment before answering: "No, there should be no risk of crib death."

This brief hesitation and somewhat cautious answer seemed loaded to me. I had promised myself that I would be less nervous for my second child, but that task was not being made easy for me!

---

[1] Ductus arteriosis – The connection between the aorta and pulmonary arteries present during fetal life which usually closes shortly after birth.

Prof. Sapiero then suggested a fluoroscopy, a special X-ray showing direct movement of the heart and lungs.

"I would like to know," he said, "what the fluoroscopy will reveal about that invisible right lung." Relieved as I was to know that the heart was normal, I'd forgotten all about the mysterious invisible lung! Perhaps because we were in a cardiology ward where cardiac malformations frighten everyone, only Anne's cardiac situation had been on my mind. And that is also what had preoccupied the doctors most... until now.

Good News and Bad News

The fluoroscopy had not yet been scheduled. Normally, I should have returned to the ground floor and waited in line once again at the cash registers in order to pay for the examination and fill out other forms. Then I would have had to find an elevator that would stop at the eighth floor, the whole process requiring that both doctors wait at least twenty minutes. Instead, Prof. Sapiero took us directly to the X-ray room, all the while assuring me that the examination would be brief and not aggressive. Indeed everything took place in only a few seconds, with great gentleness and expertise. Afterwards, however, Prof. Sapiero seemed confused. He remained silent a few moments, before speaking:

"It seems that at least one lobe of her lung is missing. It's all right, though," he added almost immediately: "Hundreds of people in France who have suffered from TB live very well even though one of the lungs has been removed. I know one who does his yard work without any problem."

I managed to smile a little, grateful for his efforts to reassure me, but aware at the same time the grave handicap he had just revealed to me.

"I hope," I said, "that Anne will be able to do more than just yard work."

He understood my anxiety and smiled kindly, but said nothing. Were we talking about a handicapped child who could cope with her limitations or about a normal child? Prof. Sapiero, who dealt with serious cardiac malformations on a daily basis, was speaking of a relatively tolerable condition. As for me, though I had lived through the last weeks with doubt and anxiety, I had remained hopeful all this would only be a false alarm and the examinations would reveal, at worst, a mild malformation from which Anne would recover.

Though the word had not yet been spoken, we were no longer speaking about a disease, but rather a permanent handicap. Without fully understanding the consequences of this condition, I realized my daughter would never be a normal child like the others. The cardiologist had, without hesitating, crossed the line when he had spoken of a "tolerable" condition.

Parents of handicapped children understand what I mean; the initial discovery of the handicap is a difficult shock. Reality, however, imposes itself on us, usually progressively, but painfully nonetheless. The suspicion of the absence of a lung had greatly tarnished the joy of learning the heart was normal. Good news and bad news! The absence of a lung, nevertheless, seemed less critical than a heart malformation. Anne, after all, breathed very well, and was not sick.

I wondered where the Lord was leading us. For now, we were hanging on the edge, balancing between the critical and the not so serious. This doubt about her lung kept me from celebrating the absence of a heart problem as I wanted to.

Prof. Sapiero explained to me that he wanted to make sense of the situation: "What surprises me," he said, "is that there is no *situs inversus*. Indeed, other organs, such as the liver and the stomach, are in their place. When the heart is the only organ to be displaced, it is often because it is malformed. But the ultrasound has just proven the contrary. This position of the heart, therefore, seems to be secondary to another malformation, probably pulmonary. We need to see what exactly is the situation with the right lung."

I agreed with him. We now had to carry on with the investigations as long as they weren't dangerous for Anne. He was thinking out loud: "Usually, we don't perform lung scans at her age, but I'll call a friend, who is a researcher at Saint-Rémi Hospital, and he'll do it. Let's call him now."

As he was heading for the phone, I wondered why scans were not standard procedure at her age. Were they dangerous? Before I could ask him, Prof. Sapiero was already reassuring me: "It is a very harmless procedure, not as aggressive as a normal X-ray... Still the technique is a little bit delicate for infants."

His friend was away doing research in England at the time. Disappointed, Prof. Sapiero assured me he would call me as soon as he was able to reach him. I wondered why he was taking care of our situation with so much diligence. Was it a case so rare that it interested him to this extent? Was he like this with all patients? Was it because I was a physician? He had spent an entire hour with me even though I had not had an appointment with him, since I had initially come for an ultrasound! At any rate, I was glad to be dealing with such a friendly team.

Unexpectedly, my time with Prof. Sapiero ended in an unforgettably comical way. He was thoughtful enough to help me lay Anne down in her bassinet, which he then took from me to carry down to the ground floor. This in itself was unexpected, but it became quite amusing when a nurse put a gift package under his other arm, probably from a patient. The package was large, and I was about to suggest taking back the bassinet, but he was already heading toward the elevators, the package under one arm and the bassinet under the other.

I followed him, chuckling inwardly. We looked like Dagwood's family on their way to visit some friends. At the elevator door, he tried to push the call button, and like the crow in Aesop's fable, he dropped his gift. A pleasant, fruity odor immediately filled the room. Liquor drenched the wrapping paper around the package and spilled onto the tiles of the hallway, spreading under our feet. I rapidly took the bassinet back from Prof. Sapiero, while he, stuttering from embarrassment, quickly went to his office and came back out with mops and a basin, and began to mop the floor himself.

What was I to do? I did not want to take the elevator and leave him in this mess! I took a mop and helped him! What a scene it had turned into! Now the Dagwood family was in full spring cleaning mode! Two residents, who had heard the noise and smelled the liquor, came, laughing, to help us. It evidently did not enter Prof. Sapiero's mind to request the service of the cleaning staff even though he was the director of a large cardiology service. He had probably learned, in his youth, to cover his own mistakes! Once most of the cleaning was finished, I said goodbye and took the elevator. I was still smiling as I left the hospital. Under such difficult circumstances, his kindness and simplicity touched me and helped me more than he could have imagined.

Once back home, I was not sure whether it was good or bad news I should share with Paul. I opted for the good news: "Anne has a normal heart!" I brandished the ultrasound report where the word "normal heart" was written in bright red letters.

"Look," I told him, as if to convince myself. "They wrote 'normal heart'!"

It was a beautiful day, and we wanted to share the good news with others. Several neighbors came to our back yard to ask about the results and rejoiced with us. I minimized in my own mind the importance of the pulmonary malformation, as I did not want to spoil the good news. I did, however, talk to Paul about it.

"Nothing is certain yet," I told him. "We'll see what the scan tells us. At any rate, Anne does not have a heart condition and all these awful diagnostic terms do not apply to her."

That was enough for one day.

"Therefore, do not worry about tomorrow, for tomorrow will worry about itself. Each day has enough trouble of its own." [2]

Diagnosis

Prof. Sapiero did not forget us. Ten days later, he called me to tell me of an appointment he had set for a lung scan. The examination, he said, would be performed by his friend under experimental conditions. Our case was already considered exceptional, and I did not know whether I should be glad or upset about it; Anne's case was rare enough to capture the interest of doctors and researchers. That did not bother me as long as it remained a medical curiosity and not a critical handicap.

On November 9th, Paul accompanied me to Saint-Rémi hospital in Paris. Sensing that Anne's situation was increasingly serious, he did not want to let me carry the burden of the waiting room anxiety alone. From that time on, Paul and I did our best to be together in uncertain or stressful situations. Paul always relied on me for medical judgment, but he was and still is a great source of emotional and spiritual support, a model of stability in the midst of the changing circumstances we encountered in hospitals.

Paul, who had not been present during the previous examinations, found the lung scan most difficult to bear. It was not a painful examination but the child had to be perfectly motionless. Anne was tied up with straps like a mummy from head to toe. Her one free arm was restrained with an IV. I gave Paul the task of being tender, consoling, and cuddly so I could concentrate on the technical results; the left lung was perfectly visible on the screen. The doctor told me that it looked normal. The idea that it might not be normal had not even entered my mind. I understood later that we must not take anything

---

[2] Matthew 6:34.

for granted; if one lung is malformed, you should look for a malformation on the other.

It was obvious that the right lung was showing no dye, which meant that it was not there. There was not even a lobe, nor a trace – nothing. We were, on that day, given a name for this permanent and unchangeable diagnosis: "right *pulmonary agenesis*." [3] These three words would follow Anne for the rest of her life. We had never heard of such a malformation, one of the rarest of all, with an incidence of one case out of several thousand births. In reality, figures were very difficult to establish because, until very recently even in Western countries, children who suffered from such a handicap died very quickly before a diagnosis could be established.

As soon as we were back home, I began to search for medical publications dealing with the subject. Most pediatric texts ignored it completely. I found a more comprehensive manual which briefly alluded to it, confirming that cases of *pulmonary agenesis* were extremely rare, the causes unknown and the odds of survival poor; the survival rate to the age of one year was less than 50%, and right agenesis was more serious than left. None of this was in the least encouraging.

I continued my research in the specialized periodical section at the medical school library. I learned that other malformations were often associated with *agenesis*, which explained the high mortality rate. This reassured me somewhat, since we had eliminated the possibility of a cardiac malformation. Perhaps Anne was one of the "good cases!" At the time, I had no reason to imagine that the absence of the right lung displaced key arteries, which in turn compressed the windpipe, allowing only a narrow air passage in the lower part of the airway. What could we have done had we known? Probably nothing except to worry more. Again, we needed to live one day at a time, for indeed:

> "*...each day has enough trouble of its own.*" [4]

---

[3] Right pulmonary agenesis – complete absence of the right lung.
[4] Matthew 6:34.

The diagnosis had been established. Anne was doing well, and all we could do was to live as normally as possible. I saw the pediatrician at our local hospital and asked him what I should do in case of a cold or bronchitis. He admitted that he had never encountered such a problem before and encouraged me to treat her like a normal child. Anne was two months old and her good health reassured everyone.

We experienced about twenty normal days. We took care of Anne as if she were perfectly normal, convincing ourselves that things were not so serious as they had seemed. But Anne was not thriving. At three months, she was about one kilogram (two pounds) underweight, yet was energetic. She held her head well and was discovering the world around her. Her smiles cheered our hearts.

Matthieu seemed to adapt to her and sometimes lay down beside her on the bed with his arm around her as if to protect her. We were happy not to have to go to hospitals and, little by little, gained confidence.

Troubles Begin

December arrived. I looked forward to buying Anne her first Christmas present. It seemed to me that she deserved a reward for all that she had gone through. Dreaming already of our first Christmas with her, I chose a multicolored mobile to suspend over her crib, and stored it in a wardrobe until the big day.

On December 3rd, I noticed that Anne was making some noise while breathing. It wasn't a cough but an intermittent kind of purring sound. Paul and Matthieu both had bad colds, and she was probably catching one as well. As she went to sleep, the purring sound ceased, and I was reassured; I did not mention the noise to Paul.

During the night, I had an odd dream that remained in my memory for a long time. It was an exceptional dream which seemed so vivid that I had a hard time believing it was not real, even after waking up. It was not a nightmare, but rather a message that patience would be required.

In my dream, Anne became very ill and had to be hospitalized. She stayed at the hospital for three months; a terribly long time to be separated from her. Famous doctors and surgeons from around the world came to see her. Finally, after this long period, she would come back to us in good health. What struck me most in this dream was the patience we seemed to need as we awaited Anne's return, as well as the fact that world-famous doctors would be involved with her care. The next morning I did not know what to make of it. Anne had slept well. Perhaps the slight purring sound was not indicative of anything.

In reality, the swelling caused by the inflammatory reaction from a viral infection had reduced the airway to less than a millimeter, and this narrowing of the trachea was the cause of the abnormal noise. Anne could have suffocated that night, but God protected her. A great adventure began for us when it very well could have ended that night.

On December 4th, my anxiety increased. As the hours went by, I felt my stomach slowly go into knots. I had hoped that the respiratory noise, which had disappeared during the night, would not come back. On the contrary, it was becoming louder. I did not know what to do. Should I take Anne to the hospital for what was probably only a cold?

I finally decided to talk to Paul, who had noticed nothing. He trusted my judgment completely, which obviously did not help me make a decision. Feeling the need for medical advice, I decided to call the pediatrician at the local hospital. "Anne makes strange noises while breathing and it worries me," I said timidly, sorry to have interrupted his work. "Bring her to me," he said. "We'll do an X-ray. It won't take long."

Feeling that I was doing something useless, yet justified by the fact that Anne had only one lung, I left for the local hospital. We were not too worried, and Paul stayed at home with Matthieu. "It won't be long," Dr. Charles had said!

A Serious Mistake

Dr. Charles examined Anne, and heard, as I had, an abnormal sound. He sent us to the X-ray department. In the waiting room, I was hoping that my turn would come soon. Anne was very alert. Sitting on my lap, she held her head up and looked around. In this position, she made almost no sound at all, and I asked myself what I was doing here with a child who only had a minor cold and no fever. I felt like going back home. She was three months and ten days old and was becoming energetic and alert. No one could have imagined that two hours later she would be in a critical state with very limited odds of survival.

What would have happened had I not gone to the hospital? I will never know. Perhaps she would have naturally overcome the cold and never needed to be hospitalized. Perhaps her health would have worsened progressively to the point of respiratory failure. Perhaps she would have died suddenly at home.

It is pointless to try to imagine what might have happened. The consequences of my decision to take her to the hospital probably changed the remainder of our lives, but I will never know how much. Only one thing is certain; the treatment inflicted upon my daughter in the X-ray room precipitated a respiratory crisis.

The next two hours were among the most difficult in my life. I clearly recall the details of the scene. Anne was suspended by the wrists so a chest X-ray could be taken. Once informed about Anne's malformation, the radiologist decided to take pictures after introducing barium by the mouth into the esophagus. He did this to see if there might be a deviation of the esophagus, and, by contrast, of the adjacent trachea. It was a good idea, but proved very difficult. How can you make a three-month old infant swallow spoonfuls of "white plaster" on demand? I was asked to help.

Anne was attached to the X-ray table with large straps so that she couldn't move. Only her head remained uncovered, which made her look like a mummified baby. Of course, she began to cry, becoming increasingly tired. She refused to accept the spoonfuls of barium so we prepared a baby bottle of it. She took some of it, but did not swallow it at the right time. The cardiologist had to redo the procedure countless times. She spat out more barium than she swallowed. The radiologist became impatient and told me in an accusatory tone that it was very important that I make her drink the barium exactly when it was needed if he were to have clear pictures. Anne, exhausted by this treatment, fell asleep on the board. I had to wake her up every two or three minutes, whenever the radiologist told me to, so that I could give her a supplementary dose of that revolting drink. When she began to cry, I felt like telling the radiologist I could care less about his wonderful pictures, and I already had more than enough of the procedure. We had been there for over an hour already and I felt like untying her and taking her out of there.

He came back from the viewing room very excited, telling his colleagues of the excellent pictures he had obtained. He did not, of course, explain anything to me or seem to show any concern for Anne's clinical state.

I felt anger mounting, but did not dare leave or say anything. I obeyed his word despite cursing him within, suffering for Anne and feeling my fear grow. I felt alone, armed only with my love for my child, isolated before this impersonal machine, which merely created "beautiful images."

I was young and inexperienced, with little self-confidence. I would never accept this sort of treatment today. I have learned to stand firm in front of any medical authority and always give priority to my child's clinical state rather than the interest of the tests being inflicted upon her. This experience in the X-ray service was a real learning experience for me, but nearly cost the life of my child.

"One more picture." This cardiologist paced around the room. He would never be satisfied. He was acting like a gold prospector who has found a few gold nuggets and feverishly looks for more.

The ordeal lasted about two hours. Anne was crying. Her breathing was rapid and noisy, yet they would not let her enjoy her sleep.

At last it was over. The radiologists discovered a deviation of the esophagus and a narrowing in the lower part of the trachea. It was, indeed, an important step forward in Anne's diagnostic evaluation because we did not suspect this tracheal narrowing which was probably causing the respiratory noise. But what a price we paid for this diagnostic advance! Anne was now fast asleep in her bassinet, completely exhausted. I could see that she was out of breath, but I wanted to let her sleep.

Of course, we had to go see the pediatrician again. I had more than enough and began to regret having come, but at the same time, I was convinced we now had to go through with this investigation, and therefore went back to see him. I did not think much about the radiological discoveries concerning the tracheal narrowing; all I cared about was Anne's present condition. I feared the pediatrician would want to have her hospitalized. I wanted to keep my baby with me. We had never been separated. I was nursing her five times a day. She needed to gain weight and be with us. I refused to admit that she was sick!

Anguish

The pediatrician immediately noticed Anne's condition had worsened considerably during the two hours in X-ray. I explained to him that she was exhausted, that she needed to rest and that perhaps she would then breathe better. Would he let us go back home? He was not very talkative, but he did tell me to remain there with her, feed her if she became hungry and let her rest; he said he would see her again later.

A nurse took us to a small room that was glass on all four sides. I could see everyone coming and going. We were finally alone. Anne even managed to nurse a little but her respiratory state was not improving. On the contrary, she could not go to sleep anymore, despite her exhaustion. She breathed rapidly and loudly. I could see her ribs over-expanding in her effort to get air. She looked like a child struggling during an asthma attack, and my anxiety increased.

When I had left the house, it seemed as though Anne only had a cold and we were going for a routine X-ray. Now, I did not know how to inform Paul what was happening. I did not dare leave Anne for a moment to make a phone call. No one was entering the room. Who could I ask for help? What would I request? Would I ask someone to call my husband for me, or to take care of Anne for a while? I did not dare. Whom could I trust with her? I was too fearful, and besides, from where would I have called? The public telephones were on another floor, the elevator would need to come quickly, I would have to find the necessary change, the phone would have to be available... all this was much too complicated! I had to stay alone with my anguish; no, I could pray. The telephone line with God is always accessible, direct, free and immediate. That is what I did while cradling my baby in my arms: "Lord, I entrust Anne to You. Take care of her. You created her. You know her needs. You know I really do not trust this hospital after what happened in the X-ray department. Please, don't let them keep her here!"

I knew that I was not alone and I was reassured.

I promised myself I would stay with Anne if she was hospitalized. I knew mothers were sometimes allowed to stay with their babies. Since I was breast-feeding her, it would certainly be a possibility.

Anne's condition continued to deteriorate before my very eyes. She was now cyanotic and was struggling for survival. I signaled a nurse who was passing by and asked her to call Dr. Charles. Noticing the deterioration, he immediately had her arterial blood oxygen and carbon dioxide levels tested. The results came back quickly and were very alarming. Anne was not receiving enough oxygen to adequately support her brain and her heart. Carbon dioxide was accumulating instead of being eliminated by her lung. The pediatrician made a few quick phone calls, then came back to see me:

"She needs to be hospitalized in a pediatric intensive care unit," he said. "The closest university hospital is full, but there is room at Saint-Gilles in Paris. The ambulance will be here in a few minutes."

Intensive care? I had not, until then, realized the gravity of the situation. I had feared a simple hospitalization, while what my child needed was vital, intensive assistance. There was nothing I could say. The ambulance might arrive any time now. I needed to call Paul. The pediatrician told me I could use the telephone in his nearby office.

"Come quickly, they are going to take Anne to Paris in an intensive care ambulance, I need you right away," I told Paul.

I did not have time to say anything else; Anne was going at any time.

Paul dropped everything and came. Leaving Matthieu with the neighbors, he arrived just as the ambulance was leaving. Meanwhile, I had to give Anne over to the emergency physicians who took her away in a small plastic cubicle which gave her oxygen.

It is difficult to convey the heartache I felt as I put her in their hands. A part of me had been wrenched away, leaving me powerless. I could plainly see that she needed intensive care and I feared she might die at any moment. At the same time, I wanted her with me. I wanted to hold her. I wanted to be allowed inside the ambulance. I had the feeling she would not survive without me, but this was of course out of the question. She was taken out of my hands, for better or worse, by the medical corps. I informed Paul of the situation in a few seconds. Without even consulting each other or discussing the situation, we rushed to the car to follow the ambulance.

We went through forty-five minutes of anguish, a very long forty-five minutes indeed! Not knowing what was going on inside the ambulance, we feared the worst. I felt physical anguish, fear in my stomach, nausea. The ambulance ran red lights, and so did we.

Friday nights during December in the Montparnasse district – the streets are jammed and the restaurants are filling with Christmas shoppers. The ambulance was stopped in traffic, despite the blaring insistence of its siren. There was absolutely no room to pass, either on the right or the left.

I railed against the city, against the futility of Christmas shopping. I cried out to the Lord, desperately, not knowing what to tell Him! The ambulance started again, zigzagging between cars, but then the siren stopped. Why? Was it all over for Anne? What happens in such a case? Would they stop in the middle of a traffic jam to tell us our daughter was dead... in fact, I was not even sure they knew we were following them. They kept going. This meant nothing, of course, since they needed to go to the hospital anyway. The siren started up again. Perhaps she was still alive? We wanted to go faster, squeezing between blocked cars, fearing her condition had suddenly worsened?

The sign at the entrance of the hospital finally appeared. The suburban hospital ambulance drivers were not very familiar with downtown hospitals. Looking for the Intensive Care building, they went too far, hesitated, and stopped at a dead end. We stopped behind them. Was Anne still alive? I held my breath. We got out of the car, ran toward the ambulance drivers as they asked pedestrians for directions. All of this seemed insane while a child was struggling to live!

Precious time was lost. Paul and I had seen a sign indicating the entrance of the Intensive Care building. We pointed it out to them. The ambulance turned around, and we followed. The road curved between old buildings and other, more modern ones. The ambulance stopped in front of an old red brick building. Near the door, a small sign read: "Pediatric Intensive Care."

The paramedics took the small transparent plastic crib containing Anne. She was alive! She looked less blue and struggled less with oxygen. Paul, who had not been seen her since that morning, tenderly and tearfully leaned toward her. For a few seconds, we forgot we were in a hurry. We were quickly reminded!

The paramedics put the crib on a stretcher with an oxygen tank, the heart monitor, and the IV equipment. It reassured us somewhat to see her cared for in such a way. We went through the doorway. The building was old, and the paint was peeling off. There was no information desk. We took an old clattering elevator, one of those archaic machines with an iron accordion door. I could not believe this; we were really going to end up in the Pediatric Intensive Care

Unit? The elevator had not yet come down... it was stuck somewhere higher. One of us had to go up the stairway to release it. It finally came down, clanging all the way. We all hurried in. "Intensive Care, 3d floor": the sign was handwritten with a marker, surrounded by graffiti.... It took faith to believe it!

Fortunately, we did not have much time to worry about these things. The racket of the elevator doors announced our arrival to the third floor. Once we went through a set of double doors, suddenly, everything changed. The unit was new, clean, and a doctor, a friendly woman, arrived immediately: "It's the baby Dr. Charles told us about," she said. Immediately, a flurry of white gowns came to take Anne toward a hallway, which, though mysterious did not seem hostile because it represented hope. We were now in Intensive Care. Here they would know how to save her! This was our feeling as we left, exhausted, for the waiting room.

Chapter 3
In The ICU

Only the Present Counts

It was late. It had been dark for some time this December night. The waiting room was empty. We were relieved to be here, but worried! A friendly, tall intern came in. He came to ask the questions needed to open Anne's file. We were happy the doctors had taken care of Anne first, asking the questions later.

We were reassured during the process of giving details about Anne, about us, and about recent events. Anne was still here, alive and in caring hands. Perhaps they could save her life. This was not a certainty, but a vague relief, that was barely able to surface on our sea of fear. The calm demeanor of the nurses was comforting. As long as they talked about Anne, we knew that she was still alive! Time came to a halt for us in this waiting room. We were in a daze, calm, though not confident. Once alone again, we said little, but were happy to be together during these difficult circumstances.

Seven years previously, we had made a commitment to each other "for better or for worse." The "worse" had now come and it was good we were two, to support each other.

Someone arrived. The fear of bad news returned, but the staff was merely inviting us to come see Anne. We entered the unit for the first time. While the waiting room seemed disconnected from time, the Intensive Care unit was truly a world apart. Only the ward's medical workers usually are allowed to penetrate into it. Parents are admitted if they are given permission by a doctor, who first informs them of the condition of their child.

Everything was new to us as we entered the unit, but we had no desire to be curiously looking about. We wanted to see Anne alive and nothing else mattered much to us. We went into separate dressing rooms, where we were to don gown, cap and face masks. I rigorously followed the instructions on the wall, washing my hands up to the elbows, after removing my rings and watch.

This small ritual soon became a familiar habit, like a daily border crossing into Anne's country. More than a simple rule to ensure hygiene, it was also a psychological preparation. When a parent goes through the ICU dressing room, he leaves the rest of the world behind to penetrate into the privileged universe of the patient. The parents, the only ones to be admitted into this universe beside the staff, are privileged indeed. They are the only ones able to see the child. We appreciated this rule. In these circumstances, we did not want to share Anne with others, even our friends or relatives. A form of complicity gradually developed between the medical team and us, tending to exclude outsiders.

This first evening, I washed my hands as carefully as if I were about to perform a surgical procedure myself! I wanted everything to go according to the rules, giving Anne every possible chance. I wanted a conscientious and caring staff. I wanted structure, limits, and rigor that reduce the chances of human failure. This I found in this Intensive Care Unit, and I felt reassured.

Under different circumstances, Paul's masked surgeon's outfit would have made me laugh. We followed the nurse guiding us toward Anne's room. The regular noise of the ventilators and the intermittent ringing sound of the monitors form the background noise of the ICU. Although there could be as many as 16 children in the unit, no noise, cries or laughter could be heard. Most children were intubated [1] and could emit no sound. Some were unconscious and many were tiny infants, often tiny "preemies" in their incubator. On this 4th of December, the noise made by the machines was not

---

[1] Intubated – the procedure where a breathing tube is inserted into the windpipe.

yet familiar but I barely noticed it. To be truthful, I had never seen
an intubated infant, even after eight years of medical studies and a
doctoral thesis in ENT! [2]

The nurse led us to the third room on the right, a large single
room, glassed on all sides. All the rooms in this unit were thus
designed, enabling staff to keep an eye on several children at once,
yet keeping them isolated from one another. That evening, however,
we only had eyes for Anne. She alone occupied our thoughts.

What struck me most was to see her, so tiny, in a large bed. She
was lying on the end of an adult bed, completely naked and connected to all sorts of wires. She reminded me of a butterfly pinned
by itself on a large bulletin board. Nothing surprised me, neither the
wires nor the large bed, as I was convinced that everything was
designed perfectly and according to a well-determined plan. I would
later question that confidence, but today my trust was complete,
absolute. I immediately noticed that Anne was struggling less than
before, she was breathing air enriched by 40% oxygen. The doctor
on call, a young woman, explained to us:

"Her condition might be explained by a viral episode she did not
tolerate well because she has only one lung. We will know more as
soon as we obtain the results of the lab tests. We started an intra-
venous to administer antibiotics. With the oxygen input, her condition could improve very quickly. However, you should count on her
spending about ten days here."

We absorbed her words as gospel truth. It was the first and last
time the staff would say anything to us about the time frame of her
stay.

We did not know enough yet to ask intelligent questions, and
therefore said nothing. We were happy to see she was struggling less
to breathe, finally getting some rest. The monitor showed a very

---

[2] ENT – Ears, Nose and Throat. This medical specialty includes diseases
of the trachea.

rapid cardiac and respiratory rhythm, but, since we did not really have anything to compare it with, we did not worry.

What were we to do now? These precious few minutes allowed in her presence were ticking away. We had to admit that we were no earthly good here and could even be in the way if we stayed. The staff was very kind to us. They said, "You may call for news of Anne tomorrow morning after nine o'clock, and you may come here after three in the afternoon."

We exited the unit slowly, realizing we would be without news for more than ten agonizing hours; day and night no longer meant anything. I felt like an astronaut in space, unable to communicate with her base for ten hours. The ICU, indeed, had already become my base. Life, reality, and everything that counted were there.

As we left the squeaky elevator and went out into the cold, dark December night, fears and discouragement came back. Dark thoughts invaded my mind; what would happen if she died during the night? Did they tell parents immediately, or would we only learn the news when calling the hospital at 9:00 am? Fortunately, Paul was there to remind me that Anne was not only in the hands of competent people, but also in the Lord's hands.

Then I remembered the dream I had the night before. I was encouraged. In the dream, this trial lasted a long time and I needed great patience. This recollection surprised me, for there was no apparent reason why Anne would stay in the hospital for months because of a respiratory infection, even if it was serious. If she survived this critical stage she would improve in about ten days, perhaps a little longer, but she should at any rate be home for Christmas! I shared my dream with Paul:

"Do you think the Lord could speak to us in such a way? Was he alerting me that I would need greater patience? Or reassuring me as to the outcome of this ordeal?"

Although I had experienced profound faith since the discovery of the reality of God eleven years before, I did not have a mystical nature, and had a hard time believing God could speak through a dream or vision.

"The Lord," Paul told me, "can sometimes speak to us through dreams. But He never does it to frighten us, because He is love and

"...*perfect love drives out fear....*" [3]

God does not want us to worry about the future, either. If he speaks to us in dreams and visions, it is for our good, never to make us worry in circumstances in which we are helpless."

"Precisely," I told Paul. "This dream was not really frightening, it was rather an indication we were going to need much patience...."

"Maybe we will need a great patience! That is actually a good sign; it means she is going to live, which is what we so dearly want. We have no objective proof this dream comes from the Lord, but in any case, He allowed you to have it, to feel it intensely, and there could be a reason for that."

This conversation on the return trip home helped reduce my anxiety. I could detach myself from the present situation for a little while to catch a glimpse of God's perspective.

We arrived home. Matthieu was spending the night at the home of friends. There was nothing left for us to do, except to trust God and pray, which is precisely what we did that night. Finally we went to bed late into the night. Much to my surprise, sleep overwhelmed me. I, who had suffered so many sleepless nights before Anne's birth, when I had nothing to fear, went to sleep on this dramatic night, confident in the Creator's love. I was already beginning to learn a very important lesson: God's grace is available to us when we need it most and at just the right time when we ask him.

---

[3] I John 4:18.

Life Hanging by a Thread

Our blind trust in the ICU's exploits was short-lived. When we visited Anne the next day, she was struggling again. It was hard for us to watch her. She was blue, her shoulders lifting with each respiratory effort, using all her energy to catch every small breath of air. Her small naked body on this large white bed struggled with all its might – her ribs expanded every second, then contracted immediately. How exhausting it seemed! How much longer could she struggle like this?

Suddenly, we painfully realized that no human intervention, even the most sophisticated, would be certain to save her. We were distraught. The doctor on call whom we had seen the night before was no longer there; the ICU's reassuring atmosphere of the night before seemed to have evaporated. This afternoon, everything was in turmoil, and we felt disoriented. The doctors and nurses were, of course, not the same ones as previously on duty. They do not work 24-hour days. No one knew us or paid attention to us; we were lost.

As we entered the dressing room, a doctor came to talk to us – or was it a nurse? How could we know? They did not wear name tags on their blouses which were all the same color. We would have liked to speak to the ICU chief, but in our own confusion, we were incapable of asking to whom we were speaking.

"Are you Anne Sanders' parents?"

"Yes," we answered fearfully, dreading he might announce to us her death during the night.

"She's under a high concentration of oxygen. It may be necessary to intubate her, if her condition worsens."

Seeing Anne in such respiratory distress, I desired even more strongly to see the doctor in charge. But no one entered the room, all we could see was a number of very busy white gowns moving in the hallways. I wanted to tell them: "Hurry up, intubate her, do something, can't you see she is going to die? She is exhausting herself!"

But I said nothing and I would not have said anything even if I had seen the head doctor. Surely they must know what they're doing. How powerless we feel!

Why were they so hesitant to intubate Anne if it could help her improve? The doctor told us he would do it if her condition worsened, but right now she seemed to be doing so poorly! Why was an intubation so dangerous? Did they not perform such procedures every day? Patients undergoing anesthesia are usually intubated. Why were they letting her suffer like this?

I did not know at the time, and no one was there to explain it to me. Intubation represents a very important act in intensive care, a decisive step in the therapeutic process. An intubated person can only be cared for in the ICU. It is the logical step taken preceding ventilation by machine, with all its complications. It is especially difficult to wean the patient from the breathing tube. One knows when to intubate, but it is much more difficult to know when to extubate! [4]

We stayed alone in Anne's room; we had been allowed to enter, but no one ever came in while we were there. We were not familiar with the myriad of ICU instruments. How I wished a nurse would come and explain everything to us! Perhaps they knew from the chart that I was a physician, and thought that I was already well informed. How wrong they were! I had never done an internship in intensive care during my studies, and I knew almost nothing about it. Most of all, she was my child who was struggling for her life and I needed above all to be assisted, as would any mother watching her child struggle for life.

I had an overwhelming desire to take Anne in my arms, to cuddle and kiss her. That was out of the question. She was still "pinned" onto that large white bed, attached by the wrists and ankles, wired from every part of her body. We did not even dare touch her. No one told us whether we could touch her or not. It was such an effort of

---

[4] Extubate – the process of removing the endotracheal, or breathing, tube.

self-control to look without touching. I learned later that all this self-control was wasted effort; nothing should have kept me from caressing her between the many IV tubes, bandages and restraining bracelets.

We did not know. We did not dare. We were alone, with the increasingly clear sense that the staff was avoiding entering the room while we were there. We noticed them through the glass walls, entering other rooms very often, and we hoped to see someone come in and answer our questions, guiding us through this still unknown world of intensive life support. But no one came. Our eyes went from the small body struggling to breathe to the monitor whose respiratory and cardiac rhythms were much too rapid.

We did not stay long. Anne did not seem to recognize us. She was only three months old, and her state of consciousness was altered by her critical respiratory situation.

We silently left the room and the ICU, not knowing what to say to each other, not even knowing what to think. We were powerless inside her room and powerless outside of it. We would not be well anywhere, as long as Anne was unable to breathe restfully.

This visit troubled me greatly. I wondered if the doctors were really in control after all. The previous evening, we were informed of Anne's diagnosis, the treatment plan and the length of stay in the ICU. Now, there was only a brief comment about her immediate state and the possibility of aggravation. Suddenly, only the present mattered. We had to reprogram our minds to exclude thinking about the future. It was a remedial course for me; I who liked to make plans. I had to resist the temptation to think ahead. I could not take life for granted. Who could tell if Anne would be here tomorrow? Never before had the verse in James' epistle struck me as much as it did now:

> *"Why, you do not even know what will happen tomorrow.*
> *What is your life? You are mist that appears for a little*
> *while and then vanishes."* [5]

---

5   James 4:14.

Outside the hospital, life was unbearable. It was obvious I could not call every hour for news of Anne, but how could I live without knowing? My despair was overwhelming. Inside the room, I could not stand the pitiful sight of my child; outside the room, it was even worse. I now wanted to return to the ICU. But why? Anne would not recognize me. I would not be able to take her in my arms. No nurse would talk to me, I would only be in the way, I would not know where to go to keep from bothering the staff. At that time, reason won out over feeling; I had to go home and discipline myself to hear news only at scheduled times. I had temporarily forgotten the tremendous power of prayer and the grace of God. But He had not forgotten me. He would walk with me day by day, and, against all odds, life would go on, be tolerable, under the most difficult circumstances.

Intubated!

On December 6, forty-eight hours after being admitted into the unit, Anne was intubated during the night. This procedure involves inserting a catheter – a small plastic tube resembling a drinking straw, except more flexible – into the child's airway. This is done by using a laryngoscope, an instrument resembling a metal tongued blade with a light shining at one end. It is a delicate procedure, theoretically reserved for anesthesiologists and ICU doctors, because it can cause grave side effects if not correctly performed.

Anne's intubation was not simple because of her tracheal malformation. Did this first intubation damage her windpipe? We will never know, because it was not possible, during the bronchoscopies that were later performed, to differentiate between congenital malformations and lesions possibly caused during treatment. Still, it really would have made no difference.

Anne's intubation had two major consequences: First of all, her condition improved immediately as soon as the tube was installed. In the long run, however, the very presence of the tube caused damage to the mucous membranes which made it impossible to extubate her after that first viral infection. The doctors themselves could not be completely aware of Anne's high risk when they made the decision to intubate her. They probably had no choice, considering Anne's critical respiratory condition.

On the morning of December 6, when a doctor announced to us by telephone that Anne's clinical state had progressed dramatically, it seemed like excellent news. Yet we sensed some reservation in the doctor's tone of voice. When I arrived in the unit that afternoon, the new doctor on call explained to me that his colleague from the preceding night had no choice but to intubate Anne, but I felt very clearly he wished the operation had not been performed. I did not understand why and he was not very clear. I then did not yet know enough about Anne's problems to ask specific questions.

When I saw Anne, I was very relieved to see she was no longer struggling. She was resting rather peacefully on the bed. The therapeutic paraphernalia was much more imposing than the previous day. Anne was on the ventilator, her breathing supported by a machine, bringing a mixture of air and oxygen through the tube. Her respiratory rhythm was regulated by the machine. We could see Anne's chest expand at the same time the piston of the machine moved. The breathing tube entered one of Anne's nostrils, while a feeding tube to Anne's stomach entered the other nostril.

I later found out the doctors disagreed about the cause of Anne's problems and about intubating her. Some physicians had suspected *tracheomalacia*, a deformation of the trachea, an abnormal flaccidity sometimes associated with the absence of a lung. Others attributed the respiratory distress to a viral infection on her only lung. The person who had intubated Anne had thought of a viral infection, while those suspecting *tracheomalacia* wanted to avoid intubation at any cost. A flaccid trachea cannot be easily weaned from the tube. Would it have been possible to avoid the intubation? This became a moot question once the procedure had been performed.

A World Apart

The Intensive Care unit is another world for the parents of children hospitalized there. For those who work there, it is only a slice of their normal lives. They come at fixed times, spend a few hours in the ICU and leave. Even if they grow attached to the children they treat, they are not their parents. They rub shoulders daily with illness and death, but it is not their own child for which they are providing care. Their lives may be touched by individual children, but not as acutely and deeply as the child's parents.

Some caregivers cannot stand close contact with death. Rare are those who remain in the stress-ridden ICU for many years. Some of those who do remain may have grown indifferent, but more often, they are people with a special calling, giftedness and compassion.

For parents with hospitalized children, the ICU represents at once both despair and hope, and becomes the dominating reality in their lives. The parent of an ICU child does not simply exit the service to carry on a normal life. They reluctantly leave because time is up, or because they can do nothing for the unconscious child. they do not return to a normal life, but live through the unit in the outside world, to which she or he no longer fully belongs.

All the mundane agitation around them seems unreal. They are surprised to see people living apparently carefree lives. Real life for them takes place in Intensive Care, where true values are – life struggling against death, love so strong yet powerless. They are surprised by the trivial mishaps that anger people. They cannot comprehend other people's irritation and anger – don't they understand that all these are so insignificant?

These two worlds coexist and touch each other but do not understand each other. For Paul and I, having Anne in Intensive Care represented a crumbling of our world, in which the past has no importance, a present is far too present, and the future does not exist beyond the next few minutes.

For this reason, keeping us anxious parents waiting ten minutes in the waiting room before giving us news of Anne was to inflict a mental torture that is difficult to imagine for anyone who has not experienced it. Ten minutes seems like nothing to the employee cleaning the room before allowing us to enter, but for us parents in the waiting room, these ten minutes were excruciating, wondering why we were not allowed to enter, while fearing, crying and feeling as if we were losing our sanity.

The first days were the most difficult for us. We were completely disoriented, recognized no one, did not know what to do with ourselves, dared not ask questions and felt out of place. We went through the motions of daily life, out of habit, as in a dream. Our minds were elsewhere, in that vital part of ourselves that was being torn away, and for which we felt powerless. We could only be present, love and pray.

For those working in the ICU, getting to know us, and speaking to us is to become vulnerable. It means letting love for that child infiltrate their soul, becoming emotionally involved, and inflicting the emotional consequences of their profession on their personal life. We cannot blame these professionals for rejecting this option. Some professionals protect themselves by speaking to parents about superficial things in a light and jovial tone. That is better than nothing. It is at least the beginning of some form of communication. Some staff even fear casual contact and wait until parents leave their child's room before providing care to the child.

Some healthcare professionals stay in the room briefly, saying little, communicating through simple acts or a few words that they are not insensitive to the parents' distress. In our experience, those professionals were relatively rare and admirable. Some, at the cost of their own personal peace of mind, grew attached to our child, and gradually entered the life of our family. Without realizing it, they transformed a medical case into an affectionate personal relationship.

Is it possible to love patients and treat them effectively at the same time? Yes, but this is a difficult task and these professional caregivers may risk being misunderstood. Those who work in Intensive Care for long periods are often capable of loving while carrying out their responsibilities. It is difficult to serve for many years in the ICU without being personally affected. These special caregivers navigate between the world of life, death and love, and the outside world. Some are able to blend home and work and carry the same faith in God to both places. This sort of person may say little, but understands. Here I would like to thank those who understood us.

Distraught and Confused

During the days and nights that followed, my life was regulated by the three moments during the day when I obtained news of Anne: at 9:30 am by telephone; at 3:00 pm by visit, and at 9:00 pm by telephone. Before and after those times, I lived for the next contact.

I continued to work four mornings a week, and took care of routine work at home, but felt more like a robot than a person. Fortunately, I had to take care of Matthieu, whose needs forced me to keep a minimum of cheerfulness and a regular schedule. At the same time, nevertheless, I lived in another world – that of Intensive Care. This world seemed more real to me, and I was gradually getting to know it better.

Every morning, awakened early by worry, I could not eat breakfast before hearing about Anne, for anxiety squelched my appetite. I impatiently waited until 9:30 am, unconsciously looking at the clock every five minutes from 8:30 on. When the time finally arrived, I was afraid to call. I told myself all parents probably called at 9:30 and that I had better wait five more minutes. Around 9:45, unable to stand it any longer, the need for news overcoming my fear, I would call. The line was often busy, and it was almost a relief, a respite of a few minutes. I would try again and a doctor would answer. I did not know who it was. It was almost never the same physician and they rarely identified themselves. This bothered me. I did not dare ask: "Who are you?" I eventually became acquainted with them, but during the first two difficult weeks, I was completely disoriented. I did not recognize their voices nor did I remember the names that I had heard before but had never seen in writing. They gave me divergent explanations of Anne's condition: one mentioned *bronchiolitis*, [6] another *vascular compression*, [7] yet another *ductus arteriosis*. [8] According to one, there was nothing to do but wait; according to another Anne needed to undergo surgery. We couldn't make sense of all this.

We felt cut off from the world, but our friends did not forget us. Each day brought letters of encouragement to our mailbox. Close friends proposed to serve as contact persons to give news to other friends by telephone, so that we would not be incessantly disturbed. A prayer chain was established in several churches in France.

One of Paul's colleagues was a personal friend of Dr. C. Everett Koop, an eminent American surgeon, a specialist in congenital malformations of children. [9] Our friend proposed to contact Dr. Koop. I did not know if this would be useful, but I accepted. Any form of support seemed precious to me. We found ourselves in a somewhat paradoxical situation: Anne had been hospitalized for two weeks in a unit in which no one had ever given me a real summary of her situation, only hasty and contradictory explanations. I had never seen the ICU chief and now I was talking to the Surgeon General of the United States in Washington, D.C., to ask his advice by telephone on a case with which he was not familiar!

I was a somewhat intimidated and surprised to hear Dr. Koop who was surprisingly a simple man and a humble Christian who was well aware of human limitations and had much compassion. He himself had lost his 18-year old son in a skiing accident. Dr. Koop encouraged us to obtain the exact diagnosis of Anne's condition. He sug-

---

6   Bronchiolitis – an inflammation of the bronchioles (branches of the tra-
    cheal-bronchial tree of smaller diameter than the trachea).
7   Vascular compression – compression of the trachea and main bronchus
    blood vessels.
8   Ductus arteriosis – blood vessel connecting the aorta to the pulmonary
    artery, which normally closes spontaneously at birth.
9   At that time, Dr. Koop was the Surgeon General of the United States.

gested we meet with the ICU chief as soon as possible in order to obtain this information. He also advised us, if the condition proved to be *tracheal stenosis*, [10] to have Anne undergo a tracheotomy, [11] and he encouraged us to be patient. Dr. Koop also gave us the name of one of his friends, a surgeon in Marseille who, he assured us, could give us more advice.

The phone call with Dr. Koop was a wake-up call for us. We would no longer be passive. I wasted no time in calling the surgeon in Marseille. As soon as I mentioned the name of his friend Dr. Koop, he gave me his full attention. Though it was already after 7:00 pm, he advised me to immediately call the ICU chief at his Paris home. I felt that calling his home would be impolite, for I had always respected the unwritten rule of not calling professionals at their home. The surgeon in Marseille persisted, and jokingly advised me in an ironical tone not to call too late, as "ICU doctors go to bed early." I thought his humor was somewhat inappropriate, but I followed his advice; the life of my child in critical condition was worth transgressing some rules of politeness.

I was determined! Now that I had spoken with the Surgeon General of the United States, I was not going to allow myself to be intimidated by the chief of a Parisian ICU. I simply looked up his name in the phone book. I called, determined because of my overwhelming need to do something for Anne, yet extremely embarrassed to be calling his home in the evening.

At the age of 29, I was still shy on the telephone. The easy solution would have been to wait until morning to request an appointment with him at the hospital. I was determined to speak with him that evening, sensing that Anne's life was at stake. Although I had never seen him, I supposed that he was in the ICU each day.

---

[10] Tracheal stenosis – a stricture or narrowing of the trachea (windpipe).
[11] Tracheotomy – surgical incision of the trachea (windpipe) for making an artificial breathing hole.

I asked to speak to Dr. Péron. The person answering the call explained that he was out of town attending a conference, and gave me the number of his hotel. I called the hotel, but his telephone was busy.

My call finally went through at 10:45 pm In a few words, I explained the reason for my call, after having apologized for calling him so late and at his hotel room. It was quite obvious that Dr. Péron did not appreciate my impertinence. He told me that my daughter had been in the unit for two weeks and he was surprised that I had not come to his office instead of calling him now!

He also told me that he had two residents directly responsible for Anne's case, and suggested I should speak with them. The conversation was over. He told me nothing about her diagnosis and I had the distinct impression he was irritated by my call. Yet what would have embarrassed me under different circumstances mattered little tonight; I had acquired some important information.

Above all else, I learned that my child's life was more important than the moods of important people. This lesson would be useful for me in the future. I also realized I could see Dr. Péron in the ICU. Had I come across him there, not knowing he was the chief? This could have been the case, since no one in the ICU wore nametags.

It was also clear from the conversation that Dr. Péron had expected me to contact him, while for me, it was he who should have taken that initiative. I had not been daring enough to brave the medical hierarchy. In addition, Paul and I, totally caught up in our personal tragedy, had not even thought of going to look for the seemingly invisible ICU head doctors, nor would we have had the necessary energy to do so. It was also an important lesson for the future, the doctors in this ICU rarely took the initiative to communicate with parents. This is regrettable, but these ICU physicians seemed too busy to do more than answer questions. Certainly, also, it is not easy to speak to traumatized parents. However, they failed to help us understand our situation, increasing our already unbearable suffering.

The following day, I asked a nurse how I could meet with the chief. She told me I had to make an appointment. In the context of the ICU, the term "appointment" shocked me, for such meetings must be agreed on several days in advance, even up to a week beforehand. How could we defy an uncertain future by ignoring the present, in which my child could die at any moment?

I agreed on an appointment for the following week. This timing challenged my attempts to resist thinking about the future. I now had to tell myself, "If Anne lives to that day...." It would have seemed more natural for the ICU chief to speak to me in Anne's room. Perhaps there were reasons. Time and distance from her immediate presence could perhaps serve to obtain clearer perspective on the course of events.

I now considered the ICU as a dichotomy, both psychologically and physically. On one side, the offices, secretaries, and the chief; in the middle, the waiting room; on the other side, the ICU with its entry point into another world. It was in the present, real, but hardly bearable. It was in this world, in Anne's room, that I finally met Dr. Maurice and Dr. Houlette, head residents for the ICU chief. Now that I knew of their existence and respective responsibilities, things were brightening up a bit. Dr. Maurice was more directly in charge of Anne's case. I arranged to see him each day. I would thus receive harmonious information coming from the same person. Dr. Maurice was, in fact, easily approachable and agreed to discuss Anne's situation with us. He even gave his opinion concerning various therapeutic possibilities, not solely restricting himself to the usual report on Anne's current clinical state. He also spent a few minutes with me daily in Anne's room. I could then ask him the questions currently on my mind.

I had taken the initiative of a dialogue with the unit in quite an unconventional way, but had been rewarded. The dialogue was open and regular, thanks to Dr. Maurice. There were more trials ahead, but the situation was not as confused anymore. I was no longer alone; now I knew with whom I could communicate.

Chapter 4
Life Is But A Breath

A nne was now intubated and the presence of the tube had immediately brought her relief. Her oxygen intake could now be reduced to 40%. [1] A few days later, the medical team tested her ability to breathe on her own by periodically stopping the ventilator. They kept the machine ready to function immediately, as Anne suffered from periodic bronchospasms, provoking temporary respiratory arrests and necessitating immediate ventilator assistance.

The monitoring scope helped keep the situation under control, for it rang when she stopped breathing. After a few days, the machine became quasi useless, and an extubation was attempted. [2]

As soon as the tube was removed, however, respiratory distress would recur. Even in an oxygen tent with an oxygen input of 100%, Anne's condition declined very quickly. After an hour, the blood gas tests showed insufficient oxygen content, with an increasing proportion of carbon dioxide. Her situation required immediate attention, and, once re-intubated, her condition improved immediately. The conclusion was simple; Anne did not need artificial ventilation, but she could not breathe without the tube. Hence, the diagnosis of *tracheomalacia* [3] was confirmed.

---

[1] The concentration of oxygen in normal air is 21%.
[2] Since the tube theoretically serves as a link to the machine, it normally becomes unnecessary when the machine is no longer used.
[3] Tracheomalacia – a flaccidity of the trachea.

Tracheomalacia

This diagnosis of *tracheomalacia* was not encouraging. Healing of *tracheomalacia* is not comparable to recovery from a viral infection. The very presence of the tube caused damage to the trachea, but was indispensable in keeping the airway open. Only gradually did we understand the implications of this vicious circle. At present, we refused to speculate on the long-term odds of survival, whether good or bad.

Our refusal to envision Anne's long-term future characterized the next few years of our lives. Our attitude was not motivated by fear, or by doubt concerning God's faithfulness for our future, whatever the outcome of Anne's disease. Rather, our attitude came from a sense of humility, a respect for things beyond our control.

Some friends would say, "You'll see, when Anne is two, when she is walking and running like the other kids, we will all be reassured." This well-meaning type of remark hurt. I did not want to allow myself to think about Anne at age two, sensing that this would be presumptuous on my part, as if I were trying to force God's hand by imagining my daughter in good health two years afterward. I was sobered by the following Scripture:

> *"You don't even know what your life tomorrow will be! ...*
> *But now you are proud, and you boast; all such boasting*
> *is wrong."* [4]

What I wanted as a parent was to take responsibility for my child and care for her as best I could, to love her now, even with her tube and electrode wires, and not because of what she might or might not become.

This capacity to set the future completely aside is a gift of God's grace, granted according to our need, reserved for us in times of dire distress. Of course, it would be abnormal to refrain from ever making plans for the future. However, when the future is set aside in this

---

[4]   James 4:14, 16 – Today's English Version (Good News for Modern Man).

way, fear linked to hypothetical events is also banished, and we are able to give ourselves entirely, body and soul, to present realities and needs. Indeed, can we ever really fear the present moment, even if it is difficult to experience? Do we not fear, rather, what we project as happening in the future? Do our greatest fears not come from our imagination?

Of course, I worried during these difficult days. I felt my anxiety physically; loss of appetite, constant butterflies in my stomach, and significant loss of weight. Unexplainably, however, my mind remained at peace. I went to sleep easily at night. On awakening, my physical anxiety was manifested by my incapacity to eat anything before my daily morning call to the hospital. At the same time, my mind remained at peace. I have never understood this strange mixture of anxiety and peace of mind, but a Scripture verse reminded me that this peace comes from God and is by nature incomprehensible, though very real:

> *"And the peace of God, which transcends all understanding, will guard your hearts and your minds in Christ Jesus."* [5]

In order to decide on possible treatments, it was necessary to know precisely the extent of tracheal damage. The ICU physicians, therefore, asked an ENT specialist to conduct a bronchoscopy. This examination entails inserting a long tube equipped with a lens into the mouth and passing it down through the airway to the main bronchi. I was astonished that such a procedure could be performed on a child weighing only four kilos (less than nine pounds), breathing poorly and dependent on a tracheal stent (splint).

The examination confirmed our fears; the lower trachea was flaccid, malformed, and tended to collapse with each breath, hindering the air from flowing freely. The right main stem bronchus was absent and the left one seemed abnormally narrow. Anne's prognosis was not good!

---

[5] Philippians 4:7.

The Decision to Act

During the night between the 13th and 14th of December, Anne suffered from frequent respiratory arrests and had to be placed once again on the ventilator. Evidently, the stent effect of the tube in the trachea was inadequate. Was it because the main bronchus, which could not be supported by a stent, was also flaccid? This was an alarming perspective. It was at that time that we learned that two famous cardiac surgeons, one from Lyon, the other from Paris, were to be consulted by the Intensive Care team on December 16. Anne's case was unique. Her clinical state worsened by the day. All possibilities for treatment, even the most unusual, had to be considered. One surgeon even suggested it would be possible to place a breast implant in the space of the missing lung in an attempt to balance the pressures inside the chest cavity. The ICU doctors remained skeptical, cautious.

The ICU doctors decided an intervention on the *ductus arteriosis*[6] needed to be attempted. Dr. Latour, a surgeon at Bichat hospital in Paris, suggested, along with the cutting and suturing of this vessel, suspending the aortic arch by means of a "sling" attached to the sternum, in order to alleviate the pressure exerted by the aorta on the trachea. He did warn us, however, that the success of this procedure could not be guaranteed.

The day of the appointment with Dr. Péron, the ICU chief, arrived. I had not yet met him personally. Though I dreaded this meeting, the gravity of Anne's condition made me want this meeting to take place as soon as possible. It was already a victory that Anne had survived until now! Dr. Péron was very friendly. He received us in his large, comfortable office, away from the agitated atmosphere of the ICU. Dr. Péron informed us of various contacts established with the most renowned French specialists, drew diagrams of proposed surgical solutions, and indicated the chosen plan, the one sug-

---

6   Ductus arteriosis – Blood vessel connecting the aorta to the pulmonary
    artery, which normally closes spontaneously at birth.

gested by Dr. Latour. He warned us again of the uncertainty of the results, and of the vital threat posed to Anne's life by such a surgery. He finally told us the date of the procedure had been set for December 22, at Bichat hospital. Anne would be transferred there by an ICU ambulance.

We really could not afford the luxury of pondering the merits of this decision. We had no choice. Anne's critical state compelled us to do something. We could not leave her under artificial respiration forever, and there was no chance this tracheal malformation would heal spontaneously. It was necessary to relieve this compression on the trachea.

We now had to make it until the 22nd of December. It was the 16th. We had six more days to wait and Anne's condition continued to worsen. The air and oxygen input from the machine were being continually increased.

Every day, I waited impatiently for visiting hours. I needed one hour each way to commute to the hospital, yet could stay only an hour in her room. I still had not held her in my arms. I saw her struggling every minute to breathe, without getting any real rest. She was semi-conscious, very tired, had a gray complexion, and was constantly sweating. How long could a young child stand such a physical struggle? She was fed by a gastric tube, but vomited several times a day and was now losing weight. She was three months old and now weighed four kilos (less than nine pounds). What would be left of my baby? How long could I stand to see Anne struggling for her life, with no real hope of improvement? I was not really ready for the answer to that question. I knew that I would live day by day. I would bear under it as long as it would take – as long as possible!

Every morning I went to work in the area junior high schools, mechanically performing an occupation that had become automatic. About 9:45 am, I would call my husband, Paul, at his work. By that time, Paul had called the hospital himself and would give me news of the past night. I was glad he made the calls to the hospital. He was on the front line, and I was grateful he was shouldering that burden for me.

On December 21, Anne was transferred to Bichat hospital in critical condition, taken by the ICU ambulance to the other side of Paris. She was scheduled to return to ICU three days after the operation, but we could tell that the nurses were not optimistic. Their silence and grave looks as Anne was taken away said much about their lack of hope to ever see Anne again. They had unwillingly grown attached to this infant whom a machine had kept alive for 17 days, and who was now leaving them.

Anne's room was sterilized, then given to another child. We no longer belonged there. Yet this room had represented the only guarantee that Anne was alive. Now that Anne had left the only place where she had some sort of identity, her existence seemed unreal to me. We could not see her in the Bichat Hospital surgical unit as visits were forbidden.

This prohibition did not anger me, for I wanted all of the security procedures to be respected. At the same time, I felt sad and helpless. Would I ever see my daughter alive again? She was already somewhere I could not reach her. Was I being prepared for a more permanent separation? I had lost the strength to pray logically, but I found comfort in God's presence. I never experienced a sense of spiritual rebellion. I could not understand, but I was firmly convinced I would comprehend later. We were not victims of the arbitrary forces of chance.

A Glimpse of Eternity

By now, I had lost all hope that Anne would be able to spend Christmas with us, and the small toy I had bought before her hospitalization laid in a closet, out of sight. Her crib was still in the bedroom, but its only occupant was a singing clown that Swiss friends had sent Anne, and which we called "the sad clown" because he seemed to be waiting for company.

On the evening of December 21, we received a telephone call from Dr. Latour. We had never met him, but we knew his reputation in cardiac surgery. It made us very happy he had taken the initiative to call us. It was an unusual humanitarian gesture for such a reputed surgeon.

His call also revealed the gravity of the situation, of which we were already well aware. He warned us, too, of the low odds of success for the operation.

"I will do everything I can to improve her respiratory state. But it is a very complex problem and an extremely risky operation with no guarantee of improvement, even if she tolerates the operation well."

We assured him that we understood the situation well and that we trusted him regardless. "I will begin the operation at about 8:00 am tomorrow morning," he said. "And I think I will be finished around 1:00 pm. Call me at that time."

This appointed phone call set the beginning of a countdown in our minds. Whatever we thought or did, these hours would inexorably pass until the moment when the life of our child would be at stake on the operating table.

We were confident of the surgeon's competence. We trusted God's sovereignty. As was our habit every evening, we had a time of prayer together, then we went to sleep, with neither rebellion nor regret. Certainly we had anxiety in our hearts, but also peace of mind.

On Tuesday morning, December 22, friends came to pray with us, and to support us in this morning's ordeal. Mel and Jan Bittner, who had helped me discover a personal relationship with God eleven years earlier, and Christine, a friend and neighbor who also wished to join us. Christine is a physician and had been following Anne's problem with much interest from the beginning.

All five of us were in the living room, praying, singing, and crying together. A mixture of joy and sadness invaded our hearts. Sadness came from grief, as we had to accept the fact that Anne might not survive; but also the joy of warmly resting in the protective arms of the Savior, the Creator of the universe. We experienced a close personal relationship with Him that morning. When our children hurt themselves, when they experience pain, do they not experience the same feeling when they come and nestle in our arms? Their pain makes them cry, but they feel reassured in our loving arms.

God's love is always available, but we sometimes forget this, until He consoles us in our ordeal and gives us peace and joy once again. Fellowship with Christian brothers and sisters is also precious; a hurting child can also be comforted by his brother or sister who takes him by the hand and brings him to the parent who "can heal everything."

"Carry each other's burdens...," [7] the Apostle Paul tells us. That morning, our burden was lighter because three friends who shared our trust in God joined us in carrying our burden to the Father, who then took it completely in hand, receiving us in our pain, our tears, our questions, and sometimes our anger.

It is not necessary to say beautiful words to support a hurting friend. To be there, to assure him or her of our affection, and to give nonverbal communication is often sufficient – a hand on the shoulder, a hug – what words can suffice in these circumstances? It is pointless to say: "Everything will be all right." This we do not know at all. The future is not in our hands, and what seems desirable to us is not necessarily best. Our assurance is based on the promise that:

> *"...we know that in all things God works for the good of those who love Him, who have been called according to His purpose."* [8]

What did we understand of God's purpose? Yet, because we knew Him, we knew things would work for our good... and Anne's good.

---

[7] Galatians 6:2.
[8] Romans 8:28.

"Your constant love is better than life itself,
And so I will praise you.

I will give you thanks as long as I live." [9]

After having sung psalms of praise – songs written over 3,000 years ago by people experiencing similar trials, with the same heart and the same God – we then spoke to God through prayer. We prayed for the surgeon, and for Anne, that she wouldn't suffer, that she would survive the operation. We prayed for ourselves, too, so that we would accept and bear the outcome of this ordeal, whatever it might be.

With our friends, there were no masks, and all was laid bare. We honestly suffered. Our friends did not pretend that everything was going to be well. We experienced a rare fellowship brought by shared trial. We read the Psalms of David together, and these words seemed to come alive for us in a very special way:

"I love the Lord, because he hears me;
He listens to my prayers.

He listens to me every time I call to him." [10]

And also:

"I will call on Him as long as I live
For You, O Lord,
Have delivered my soul from death,
My eyes from tears
My feet from stumbling
The Lord is gracious and righteous
Our God is full of compassion." [11]

We sang as well. The song that touched me most that morning was a French song I often sang to Anne at her bedside:

---

[9] Psalm 63:4-5 – Today's English Version.
[10] Psalm 116:1-2 – Today's English Version.
[11] Psalm 116:4-5 – Today's English Version.

My God is so good
He cares for me so well
This God so faithful,
Do you know He is thinking of You?
He would like to help you in your difficulties,
But come to Him just as you are.
God knows so very well
What seems so heavy to you
What hurts you and troubles you every day.
He knows your every need,
Your fear of tomorrow.
With my God, you know all will go well. [12]

That morning, we had the surprising assurance that all would go well, whatever the outcome of the operation. If Anne died, God would care for everything. Why be upset? All would go well, for her and for us.

We did not possess in ourselves such great wisdom or strong faith. Critical times, such as the ones we were experiencing, are privileged moments, helping us to turn our eyes away from the temporal things of the world that so preoccupy us, and to focus instead on eternal realities.

God rarely grants us this glimpse of eternity; rather, we veil it, under normal circumstances, with our daily busyness. In this earthly life, we cannot live as though we were in eternity, freed from material contingencies. It is probably better that these rich moments remain the exception, as they were for Joshua and the people of ancient Israel as they entered the Promised Land. These are moments when God knows that we need to see further, that we need to see the future from His perspective.

---

[12] "Mon Dieu est si bon," I-M Hörnberg, French adaptation H. Lepczynski, in: J'aime l'Eternel. Recueil de Chants de Jeunesse en Mission, Lausanne, 1976, n° 133.

*"Have I not commanded you? Be strong and courageous.
Do not be terrified; do not be discouraged, for the Lord
your God will be with you wherever you go."* [13]

It has always been difficult for me to comprehend the concept of
eternal life. It is hard for me to grasp this because I am living my life
on earth. I believe in eternal life because God assures me of it in the
Bible, and because I have experienced the truth of God's Word in
other areas of my life, such as His directives concerning marital life,
the education of children, honesty in business, and so forth. I will
only truly experience the full reality of eternal life after I die. God,
however, allows us to catch a glimpse of this reality when the death
of a loved one is imminent. It is a very deep spiritual moment that
we do not seek, but for which we can thank the Lord.

1:00 pm came. It was time to call the hospital, a time both dreaded and anticipated. I stayed in the living room, surrounded by my
friends, calmly expecting the worst. Paul bravely went to the adjoin-
ing room where the telephone was located. How I appreciated once
again, his leadership at this moment. I was glad that Paul was protecting me from potential adversity.

I tried overhearing the conversation since the door was open, but
Paul was saying little, very moved, listening without speaking. This
lasted only a few seconds. He came back with a smile: "The operation is over. Anne is in post-operative intensive care, the surgeon is
waiting for us."

This did not give us much information, but we knew the bottom
line: Anne was still alive. Or at least she was alive five minutes ago.
Surgeons and ICU physicians, whose occupations are a constant lesson in humility, cannot allow themselves to have triumphant atti-
tudes. What looks like a victory one moment can turn into a
catastrophe the next.

---

[13] Joshua 1:9.

We said goodbye to our friends and rushed to Bichat hospital. It was our first visit to this hospital, since we had not been allowed to visit Anne up to this time. That day, we would not see her either, but she would be there, alive, not far from us. During the ride to Bichat, we kept the spirit of prayer that had carried us through the morning. We spoke little, as we awaited the doctor's words, not knowing if we would be rejoicing or crying on the return home. It was about 2:00 pm and we had not eaten lunch. Time and meals had lost their importance. During these days, we no longer had a schedule, time took its own course and we were powerless to change things.

Bichat Hospital was brand new, clean and silent. As we went through the cardiac surgery unit, we saw no patients, heard no children crying. The bedrooms were completely isolated, seemingly invisible. A nurse showed us to Dr. Latour's office. He received us immediately. So this was the man who had been operating on our baby for five hours. To see him there in front of me helped me regain a sense of present reality.

He explained: "Your daughter is in post-op intensive care. I won't lie to you and say that the operation was easy. My anesthesiologist worked wonders manually ventilating her only lung while I had to operate on the same side of the chest cavity. My only access to the trachea and heart was on the left side, which is where the lung is located. The anesthesiologist had to use a manual air bag the entire five hours of surgery. This surgery was risky business indeed!"

We were filled with gratitude for this anesthesiologist whom we never met, who artificially preserved the life of our daughter while the surgeon operated within the same few centimeters of her open chest.

Dr. Latour expressed his admiration once again, "The anesthesiologist overcame great difficulties, he really did a wonderful job." From the obvious relief with which the surgeon said these words, we understood that those five hours must have seemed extremely long for him and even longer for the anesthesiologist.

Dr. Latour explained, "I was surprised to find a large fibrous mass surrounding the trachea and the aortic arch. I think the mass was at least partly responsible for the compression of the trachea, so I removed it by dissecting it millimeter by millimeter along the aortic arch. Now that this mass has been removed, the trachea and the aorta are freed from each other."

This seemed good news to us. The term "success" would not be used as long as Anne's clinical condition remained critical, but at least the goal of the operation had been achieved; Anne's trachea was relieved from this compression.

Then, I asked him what the fibrous body was. Dr. Latour didn't know. Perhaps it was the embryonic remains of the missing lung.

Dr. Latour's last words were the most pleasant to hear: "I am going to keep your daughter here for 48 hours, then I'll transfer her back to Saint-Gilles."

The day after tomorrow! We were going to see her in two days! But the day after tomorrow would be December 24, Christmas Eve! Were they going to transfer Anne, even in an ICU ambulance, in the Parisian Christmas Eve traffic jams? The ambulance would have to go through the most densely populated and commercial quarters of Paris, from its northern gates to the southwest district of the capital.

Christmas

We had planned to celebrate on Christmas Eve and decided not to change our plans. Life had to go on, with or without Anne, and Matthieu was excited about the decorated Christmas tree and the wrapped presents. We had invited my parents, but only Matthieu was truly enjoying the party. Matthieu was almost three now. It was the first time he realized that Christmas meant presents and partying, and he had been looking forward to it.

A large package intrigued him particularly. The package was too large to be wrapped. It was hidden under a blanket near the tree.

After our Christmas meal, we unveiled the marvel. It was a bright green pedal car, which Papy immediately adjusted to Matthieu's size. Our son's big blue eyes shone with happiness. He proudly distributed the presents that were under the tree. It was a good family evening.

Deep within, however, I was not there. My thoughts were in the Paris traffic jams, and I could hear, as in a dream, the siren of the ambulance. Anne was to be transferred tonight, according to the information I had received in the afternoon. How I hoped that she had survived until now, and that her transfer would go well! Perhaps I would see her the following day, Christmas Day, at Saint-Gilles.

I did not want to hope or speculate too much about Anne's future, even about tomorrow. I needed to live here normally, with Paul, with Matthieu, with my parents. I could not live for Anne alone, I needed to get used to her absence. However, I refused to get used to her absence... it would be as if part of me were absent. These thoughts ran in every direction as I helped Matthieu open his presents, as I took pictures of the party, trying to be present in the moment.

I did not take out the small gifts I had bought for Anne a long time ago. Why feel sorry for ourselves while she was absent? I did not want to take them to her hospital room either. Anne was too critical to be interested in toys. I forbade myself, with difficulty, to think about the empty crib, surrounded by a canopy of flowery cotton I had sewn. Now, I did not know what to do with the crib. I could put it in the cellar and try to forget it. No, as long as there remained the most minuscule chance that Anne would return and use it, I would leave her crib in her room.

8:00 pm – The presents were distributed and we brought out the dessert. Most French households, like ours, were celebrating at that time. At this very moment, the ICU ambulance was leaving Bichat hospital. Several motorcycle policemen were escorting it across town. The motorcycle sirens joined the ambulance sirens, disturbing this festive evening in Parisian apartments. Inside the vehicle lay the object of all this costly attention, a small baby girl weighing only four kilos (nine pounds), seriously ill, being kept alive by several people who were watching the monitor, the IV, and the respirator. All of these were, in a sense, luxuries of rich societies spending such enormous sums for a child with a most uncertain future! In several clinics close by, fetuses without any malformation were being aborted, most often simply because of personal convenience. Our world is being driven mad by its own power!

8:30 pm – Anne was back in her room in the Intensive Care unit at Saint-Gilles hospital. No one told us how the transfer went, and, not knowing the exact time at which it was supposed to take place, we did not dare call. Too bad. That night, it would have been a beautiful Christmas present! We learned the details the following day.

December 25 – As soon as we could, Paul and I went to Saint-Gilles, full of both hope and apprehension. We were welcomed with smiles. We immediately knew that things were going relatively well. When we rang the doorbell at the entrance of the unit to make our presence known, I was glad to hear someone say, "It's Anne's Mom!"

Here, I was Anne's Mom, rather than Dr. Sanders, and I was happy about that, because it gave my daughter an identity. In places other than the hospital, I was no longer really Anne's mom, since I could not walk her around, show her off, and chatter about her smiles and her progress with other moms. My friends no longer dared ask me for news. Here I found Anne in a familiar environment, to which I was gradually becoming emotionally attached.

Anne was covered with tubes; a thoracic drain placed on her chest, in addition to the rest of the usual paraphernalia. Her face was covered with adhesive tape to maintain the catheters in their places, and her arms and legs attached to the bed. Nevertheless, she seemed to be doing well. She was calm, rosy-cheeked, and, in everyone's opinion, in much better condition than before the operation. The nurse who was caring for her admitted to me that she had not expected to see Anne return.

The rate of the respirator had already been diminished, and we became hopeful. If Anne could breathe on her own in a few days, the team would try once again to extubate her, and, since the obstacle on the trachea had been removed, success seemed possible! Perhaps she would soon come home! After a successful operation, would that not be a logical outcome?

Matthieu's Problem

Since Anne's hospitalization, I was torn between Matthieu's needs and my desire to be with Anne. Perhaps another mother would have made fewer hospital visits to be able to spend more time with her two-and-a-half-year old son. One might think that Anne, only four and a half months old and not always conscious, needed me less than a little boy troubled by sudden trauma in the family.

I had never missed a single visiting day in the hospital. During these long months, I waited every day for the time when I could go see Anne in her room. For me, not to go there would have been to betray her, to abandon her. I never fought my need to be with my baby every day. Of course, I also felt guilty not to be with Matthieu, but I did not realize, in my distress, how much he was suffering from the situation.

Beginning two years before Anne's hospitalization, I had worked half time, in the mornings. I was with Matthieu every afternoon. When Anne was hospitalized, I could not stop working in the middle of the school year. I continued to put Matthieu in the nursery in the morning, but because I spent my afternoons at the hospital, I had to leave him with various friends in the neighborhood. It did not take long for us to realize that this situation did not suit him at all. He began to cry often and became sad and distant.

Paul, who was able to pay more attention to the needs of our son than I, was the first to express his concern about Matthieu's distress, revealed by the boy's sad and rebellious attitude. It seemed obvious that the situation was exceptional for this three-year old, threatening to have serious repercussions for his future. Matthieu was a shy, reserved boy. He did not make friends easily, and we hated to see him draw into himself any further.

Paul made major changes in his professional life. He set his doctoral dissertation aside. He gave up his job as pastor of a young church to undertake a pastoral role in a well-established church where his primary responsibility was to prepare the Sunday sermons.

Paul continued to teach part-time at the Nogent Bible Institute in the mornings and limited his preparation for teaching these mornings. Paul devoted every afternoon to Matthieu. In many ways, this decision was a sacrifice for him, especially since his plan had been to work hard on his dissertation that year, but Paul realized that his first responsibility was to care for and protect our children. It was a simple matter of observing God's priorities.

Paul was more at ease in work than in leisure. To dedicate himself to the psychological well-being of his son, Paul set aside his plans for an indefinite period. This decision required that he no longer put professional fulfillment first. Paul never complained about this, and was very quickly rewarded as Matthieu blossomed before our eyes.

Father and son began to develop new habits, and they established a close relationship. They sometimes went to Paris in the middle of the afternoon to see the famous Guignol puppet show at the Champ de Mars at the foot of the Eiffel Tower. At other times they took the elevator to the top of the Tower. They watched the mice run along the tracks of the Paris Métro. This relationship of love and confidence gave Matthieu a sense of security, and I am convinced that these months spent in a privileged relationship with his father had positive consequences, benefits we are still reaping years afterward.

How grateful I am that my husband was able to assume these responsibilities at that critical moment and to discern essential priorities! I appreciated the fact that Paul set aside his professional objectives for Matthieu's dire needs, to come to the rescue of our family in distress.

God gave children two parents. I am so glad for that! How could I have dealt with this situation alone? To abandon my daughter would have been unbearable, and to leave my son to the care of other people, however compassionate they might be, would have caused great emotional damage to him. Matthieu found security with his father. That certainly was worth delaying a dissertation and setting aside classes, conferences, and church meetings!

Encouragements and Discouragements

After her return to Saint-Gilles Hospital, Anne's condition improved daily. She no longer had respiratory arrests. Oxygen and respirator rates were gradually lowered. Three days after her return, she was fed by a gastric tube once again, thus she no longer needed her IV. Each day, she looked a little more like a normal infant. Every afternoon, I sat next to her bed on a stool and I caressed her hand while talking to her softly, and singing songs of hope and love. Although she was now rosy and in better condition, she was still connected to various machines by electrode wires, a gastric tube and a tracheal tube. I had not yet thought I could pick her up, however. One day a nurse asked me very naturally: "Would you like to take her in your arms?"

What a question! I was dumbfounded for a few moments, looking at my daughter, covered with tubes, and then looking at the nurse, who had just talked to me as if we were in a daycare center for healthy children.

"Can I?" I asked.

"Yes, wait a second, I'll give her to you," she replied.

She lifted Anne from the bed and put her in my arms, and all the wires followed. The tubes of the respirator were long enough so that I could take her. My daughter was in my arms, for the first time in weeks! What a wonderful moment! What a sense of frailty at the same time! I immediately realized that she did not hold her head as she did before being sick. I did not worry too much about it, it seemed normal that she would have regressed in her psychomotor development, but it made me more aware of her fragile condition.

Anne seemed so light. Though she was more than four months old, Anne barely weighed more than a big newborn. Yet she looked at me and smiled, and her life then became as real to me as if she were twice as heavy, and breathed on her own. When I found Paul in the waiting room, with Matthieu, I shared my joy with him. Paul went into the ICU and also held Anne in his arms for a few minutes.

A few days later, I had another happy surprise. As I arrived in her room, I saw my baby with clothes on for the first time! She had always been naked until now, wearing only a diaper. Considering the number of medical accessories on her body and the high temperature in the ICU, I had thought that it was the norm in intensive care. I then noticed that the nurses were very sensitive to the need to "humanize" the children, as soon as their condition allowed for it. They liked to dress them nicely. This gesture did me good that morning. Anything that brought Anne closer to the world of normal children made me so happy!

Chakib Arrives

The arrival of Chakib, a new infant, in the unit was like a sunbeam to us. He was born in Casablanca on January 2. Shortly after his birth, he had suffered from respiratory distress, and his mother had done everything she could so that her newborn could receive adequate care. Chakib had been intubated in Casablanca, then transferred to Paris by plane. His mother had left her daughters in the care of their father and grandmother and had come to Paris with Chakib.

Without knowing who she was, I admired Chakib's mother. I noticed her calmness as soon as I met her for the first time in the waiting room while we both waited to be admitted into the unit, which I first mistook for unconcern. Usually, a sad silence reigns in that place. The parents who are there together rarely communicate, as they remain locked up in their own grief, and wait with anguish until admitted into the ICU, where doctors give them the latest news of their child.

Since I arrived early in the afternoon, I was often the only parent, which was a relief for me. That day, arriving at 3:00 pm as usual, I rang the doorbell at the entrance of the unit. While I anxiously waited for someone to open the door, I looked as doctors and nurses went to and fro in the unit. Were there, by any chance, many near Anne's room... I became terrified... what was happening?

After ringing the bell, it took a long time for someone to come to the door of the ICU. I was very worried. A nurse finally arrived and told me to go in the waiting room for a few minutes and that a doctor would come see me there. This situation was the worst possible torture. Had Anne passed away? No, I told myself, they would have called me. But what if they had not been able to reach me, since I had left home over an hour ago? Perhaps Anne is simply doing worse and they want to warn me. Or are they only cleaning her room? Wouldn't they have told me that to reassure me? I prepared myself for the worst. I saw interns passing by, greeting me with a nod, without coming to talk to me. Wasn't it the assistant chief's responsibility to announce the death of a child to his or her parents? Unending minutes went by. Did I still have a little girl or not? Had they forgotten me? Yet, if they were about to announce a death, how could they forget the parents that long?

I was in that state of mind when two elegant ladies came and sat down in the waiting room, chattering as casually as if they were at the beauty shop. One of them, quite lovely and about thirty years old, was evidently from abroad, currently staying in Paris. "I haven't seen Barbie dolls for the girls yet. I didn't see any at the Bon Marché. Do you think I will find that at Printemps?" [14]

This conversation troubled my morbid thoughts, and I felt as if they were profaning a sacred temple. Didn't they realize where they were? This young woman, however, seemed friendly, and her chat-

---

[14] Au Bon Marché et Au Printemps are famous Parisian department stores.

tering brought me out of my dark thoughts for a little while. Surely she couldn't be the mother of an ICU child hospitalized, with her casual attitude? Perhaps she is an aunt or a friend? But what is she doing here, where only parents are admitted? It was my first direct encounter with Maria, Chakib's mother, who later became my friend.

The assistant chief finally arrived, and, after apologizing for having kept me waiting, told me that Anne no longer needed the assistance of the respirator. She was now listed as "unassisted ventilation." She was still connected to the respirator for the sake of security, though it wasn't being used. She was breathing on her own!

After having prepared myself for the news of Anne's passing, I felt fully alive once again. Why had they not told me right away that Anne was doing fine? Was it because they wanted to let the doctor announce the good news himself? He was so busy that he did not realize how anguished I was. He had kept me waiting for over half an hour. Nurses are not responsible for giving medical news to parents, yet just a few words would have spared me 30 minutes of anguish. "The doctor is going to talk to you about Anne's treatment, he is busy right now, wait just a little bit, please...." I would then have understood that Anne was still alive, and that the doctor simply was not yet available.

Chapter 5

The Spirit of God...
The Hand of Man

I understood that this young, carefree woman was the mother of a hospitalized child, because I saw her arrive every day around 3:00 pm, like me. We were usually alone at that time and we would exchange a few words in the waiting room. She looked on the bright side of everything and that encouraged me. Her son suffered from a paralysis of the vocal chords. He would have died of asphyxia if he hadn't been immediately intubated. Now, he seemed safe as long as the tube was kept in its place, allowing him to breathe normally.

This ailment is familiar to specialists, and if it is treated in time, with intubation, it usually heals by itself in three to six months. This time period, of course, seems very long for a mother yearning to bring her infant back home, but Maria was just happy that her child had been saved, as she had lost her first son the year before. She was not really as carefree as she had seemed. Every day, she took great interest in her son's condition, helped care for him as much as she could, and discussed with the doctors the tests to be undertaken. Our new friendship soon helped both of us to pass the long hours spent in the hospital. These first days of winter, Anne's condition continued to improve as a result of her operation, and I was in good spirits. These few days of respite, however, went too quickly. A new ordeal awaited us.

On January 4, Anne was breathing well with only a tracheo-nasal tube. The ICU team decided to try to extubate her. This is done very quickly and easily, by pulling on the small tube coming out of the nostril. Some babies actually extubate themselves by accident, which is why their hands are restrained, tied to the frame of the bed. Anne had been improving since the operation at Bichat, which released her trachea. We all hoped for success that would permit us to take her home. We were in for a cruel disappointment. From the very first minutes of the extubation, Anne struggled to breathe. She turned blue and her whole body fought for air. Ten minutes later, she was in critical condition and the team reintubated her. The improvement was immediate. The diagnosis was evident. Her respiratory distress was due to tracheal collapse during expiration, because of the flaccidity of the windpipe.

As we had feared, the windpipe had been damaged by compression of the aorta. The compressing mass had been removed during the operation, but the trachea remained too flaccid, collapsing during expiration, thus lowering the internal air pressure. The doctors decided to wait two weeks before attempting a second extubation. Some, however, were already talking about a very long period of time. We did not know what to think after this sudden failure.

Anne was allowed to breathe on her own again, with only the tube, since she had previously done so well without the machine. As early as the next morning, however, her condition was not as good as before the extubation attempt. I spent several hours at her side, on the lookout for the slightest change. I noticed she was less alert and seemed to struggle to breathe.

The doctors noticed the progressive worsening of her condition later on that January day. Anne suffered several life-threatening respiratory arrests. She would stop breathing completely, become gray, and if the arrest lasted more than a few seconds, her heart would slow down dangerously. The alarm would then ring and the ICU doctors hurried to ventilate her manually, "re-starting her" like a mechanical toy functioning imperfectly.

These arrests occurred more and more frequently, and the ICU staff then decided to put her on respiratory assistance once again. It was a new blow to our morale: one step ahead, two steps back... would it ever end?

New Aggravation

Difficult days followed as Anne's condition worsened. The doctors admitted to us that the chances of her survival were very poor. Artificial ventilation was increased, as well as the concentration of oxygen. We did not take her in our arms, as we feared that this would trigger another respiratory arrest. The nurses frequently suctioned the secretions in her tube, but they dreaded this procedure, which could also trigger respiratory arrests.

One of the nurses had particularly taken Anne's case to heart. She only suctioned her in the presence of a physician, so that he would be there in case an arrest occurred. Indeed, such a crisis required immediate action. If Anne's breathing was not restarted quickly, the heart would slow down and eventually stop. Her brain would suffer damage after three minutes. At that moment, even if the child were resuscitated, permanent brain damage would have occurred.

Claude, a friendly and conscientious nurse, had been working in the unit for seven years, and knew perfectly well what could happen. She also knew that in Anne's case, the chances of survival were very slim. Far from being discouraged, however, Claude was a model of professional conscientiousness and vigilance. Each nurse was responsible for three patients. The bedrooms are all glassed in, so they can watch a child from another's bedroom, as well as from their nursing station located between the three rooms. When they do not have a particular task to perform, they do a round in each room at regular hours and are alerted by automatic alarm in case of an emergency.

When Anne was at her worst starting from January 5, we were so fortunate to have Claude responsible for her room during the night. With hindsight, I really believe God was intervening in the situation. There were four shifts of nurses, four different nursing stations in the unit, involving at least twenty nurses in all. The fact that Claude took care of Anne those nights probably saved her life. Refusing to return to her nursing station or converse with the other nurses during her night shifts, Claude stayed in Anne's room, on the lookout for any sign of change, calling the doctor as soon as Anne arrested.

The careful attention she gave Anne earned Claude criticism from some of her colleagues. I later learned that these had been very difficult moments for Claude. Some said she was doing this because the mother of the child was a doctor, or because she was trying to make a good impression on the head nurse. Did it ever enter their minds that she might have been simply trying to save the life of a child? When, much later, I heard about this conflict in the unit, I was outraged. It wasn't that the other nurses were doing their job badly, but most of them only did their usual job. Claude did more than that, for she gave part of herself. Her rigor, her skill, her professional conscientiousness, and her refusal to be influenced by criticism were admirable.

In the night between the 7th and 8th of January, Anne suffered an arrest so serious that it necessitated cardiac massage. At six in the morning, she had yet another arrest, and two different times Anne's heart slowed down so much that it became quasi-ineffectual. Once again, the very rapid response of the doctors permitted them to "jump-start" her.

Sometimes, several children need urgent care at the same time. During the day, several physicians are often on duty, but during the night, the one who is on call has to manage everything alone with his resident and the nurses. He then needs special discernment to distinguish in seconds between an emergency that cannot wait from the one which can wait a few minutes. When the heart stops, it cannot wait. When this stoppage happens more and more often and the cause of the problem cannot be treated, the odds of survival inevitably become very low.

When I saw the resident the morning of the 8th, he looked discouraged, "We saved her again, but the time will come when we won't be able to keep her going anymore." I then understood that they themselves did not really believe in Anne's chances. The cause of her respiratory arrests was unclear. I was told that they were probably due to a flaccidity of the left main bronchus as well as that of the trachea. It was impossible to put a stent in a bronchus. There was nothing to do, and it could be expected that one of her crises would soon be the fatal one.

These thoughts occupied my mind for the rest of the day, but I did not give in to feelings of helplessness. I remembered that a few days earlier, we were rejoicing about her progress and had attempted an extubation because she breathed on her own, spontaneously, with her tube. What had happened? I had the uncomfortable feeling that the doctors were not trying hard enough to understand.

There were certainly many other cases demanding treatment, just as urgent and critical as Anne's. I, however, had only one case to keep in mind and I was resolute in finding a solution, to refuse defeat in this seemingly hopeless situation. I once again had the same impressions as I had had the first days that Anne was hospitalized: No one really knew what to say; people avoided me in the hallways; every day a different resident brought me news; no one really gave as much thought to her case as was needed. We had to try to understand the cause of this sudden relapse. An idea came to my mind; could it be that the tube inserted after the intubation attempt was too short? This would explain the relapse, which had occurred precisely after this tube had been reinserted.

I tried to make some sense of the flow of my thoughts. If Anne's trachea was too flaccid down to the *carina*, [1] she would need to be intubated covering the entirety of this zone, all the way down. Otherwise, there would remain a segment of the trachea that might collapse and cause a respiratory arrest.

I had never yet dared share my views with the doctors. I had felt too incompetent until now. Now, however, I feared that a simple story of "plumbing" could take my daughter's life away. I therefore gathered all my courage and talked to the resident on call about it. He was friendly, but did not take my ideas seriously, and let me know that I was quite naive to believe in such a simple solution.

---

[1]   Carina – the distal end of the trachea, where the two main bronchi begin.

He said, "We wish the solution were that simple, but tracheomalacia is a complex phenomenon. It is very likely that her main bronchus is flaccid as well, and there's nothing we can do about that."

I asked, "But then, why was she doing well before the attempt to extubate her?"

He replied, "Tracheomalacia is an unpredictable phenomenon, we don't know why tracheo-bronchial spasms occur at certain times, and not at others. It is true that she had days of improvement, but now, the bronchospasms trigger serious respiratory arrests. The only thing we can do is to 'restart her' each time."

I replied, "But what if we tried to insert the tube a little bit further, to see if she improves?" I felt that I was starting to irritate this tall bearded fellow with my naivete and my persistence. But it didn't matter, for I had to try to convince him.

He responded, "Ma'am, we would like to believe, like you, that there is a simple solution. But the tube is placed at the same position as before the extubation attempt. It goes down to the *carina*, so we can't go any further."

What else could I say? I kept quiet, but I was not convinced. Perhaps it was a question of millimeters? On the other hand, his hypothesis that the collapse might also be located lower, on the bronchus, was plausible, and not reassuring. I had difficulty in accepting that this hypothesis could only be verified after this new extubation attempt. I thought the team should still try to push the catheter a little further down. But how could I ever convince them?

On January 8, while Paul and I were at Anne's side, we witnessed for the first time one of her most serious arrests. Despite the assistance provided by the machine, Anne's chest suddenly stopped expanding. The cardiac monitor, after having accelerated to a very high rate, slowed down dangerously. Her small "engine" was exhausting itself, lacking sufficient oxygen. The monitor alarm rang loudly for a time that seemed like an eternity. However, Sylvia, the resident on call, rushed into Anne's room, still putting on her blouse: she had been called while she was out of the unit, but in a few seconds Sylvia was at work.

We immediately left the room to let her work with the nurse and returned to the waiting room, our hearts beating wildly. A few long minutes later, Sylvia came back, with a smile reflecting both sadness and compassion, "We were able to save her again." Then, coming toward me, she affectionately put her hand on my shoulder: "I know, my poor dear, it's so hard...."

These few words, her simple gesture touched my heart. Sylvia was a skilled practitioner, but also a woman, a mother, and at that moment, a sensitive person who shared our suffering.

Anne's condition had become extremely grave, even though the ventilation pressure had been increased on the machine, and oxygen was delivered to her at 100%. Her blood gases had worsened, meaning that the oxygen did not reach the blood cells adequately. The air remained trapped in her only lung, as revealed by a major distension of that lung on the X-ray. Her gas exchanges could not take place; the circulation of her air blocked by some tracheo-bronchial obstruction. The major increase of carbon dioxide in her blood had plunged Anne into a state of semi-consciousness. She looked pale and gray.

Hopeless...

As I entered Anne's room on January 9, I received a shock. Anne now had a tracheotomy. I had been told that this procedure was rarely if ever performed. Evidently, the doctors had come to the conclusion this should be attempted, despite Anne's critical condition. I was told that it was the ICU chief, Dr. Péron, who had decided to attempt an emergency tracheotomy, in order that Anne could be more effectively ventilated. I asked, with hope, whether the trach tube could be introduced further down into the trachea. The doctors answered, that on the contrary, the tube did not go as far down as the previous one, since it was only about three centimeters long.

Now I was completely baffled. How did these doctors hope to improve Anne's breathing if the trachea was not even entirely stented? I felt that Anne's team was working blindly, without logic. If they would only look at her record since the operation, wouldn't they conclude, as I had, that only a longer tube could be the solution? My efforts to convince them to lower the tube had been in vain, since they had chosen to do the exact opposite!

When I left her room on the evening of the 9th, I had lost almost any hope of saving Anne. I was not angry and I tried to convince myself that they knew what they were doing. Yet I remained terribly frustrated. They had not even tried to put down a longer tube. She now had a tracheotomy with a short tube and her condition continued to worsen. I did not think Anne would survive the night.

We waited at home for the phone call that would announce the end, while thinking, sadly and calmly, about how we could tell Matthieu that his little sister would not come back home, and how we would prepare the funeral. We wished for a very simple ceremony in which we would testify that God's grace had never left us, even at the worst times. We felt supported, carried by an invisible force that did not take the sadness away, but allowed us to live through it in peace.

Sunday, November 10 – We were still waiting for the telephone call. We did not go to church that morning, because we did not want to be away from the telephone. Paul and I did not want to be separated either. That afternoon, for the first time, I did not go to the hospital. I did not want to take the train to Paris and be unreachable by telephone. I did not want to arrive at the hospital and find Anne dead. I preferred we be told of her death together, at home.

That evening, we still had heard nothing from the hospital. In spite of my immense desire to obtain news of Anne, I could not gather the courage to call. Paul called. Anne was still alive, but her condition was very poor. Her therapeutic escalation continued; she was now "curarized," meaning she had been artificially paralyzed with a substance called curare to allow for completely passive ventilation.

This was a more efficient method because the ventilator did not have to struggle against bronchial collapse.

I picked up the telephone. Paul and I had lost any hope to save Anne. We felt the situation resembled a sort of therapeutic relentlessness, a hopeless situation that only artificially prolonged her process of death. Did it make sense to artificially paralyze a child just to make her breathe artificially? With what hope, what future? How long? We did not want Anne to agonize pointlessly, nor did we want human techniques to delay what we believed to be God's simple plan.

I told Dr. Houlette my feelings in this regard, that we accepted her impending death. His response was very gentle and understanding, "It's true that the situation is very critical, but we cannot decide at this point to stop trying... What should we do? Stop the respiratory assistance? We have to continue on, even if there isn't much hope."

His answer gave me some energy again. How could I have given up? These men and women, fortunately, were still resisting Anne's death. Of course it was easier for them in their professional roles to keep their composure than it was for me. It was a good thing I was not the one making the decision to stop the machines.

Paul and I prayed, entrusting the situation in the doctors' hands, but counting on God's supervision. If Anne were to die, we would not be surprised, since we were expecting that outcome. If Anne were to live, it would be even better, even if the ordeal must last a long time. In the first case, she would be happy with the Lord, delivered from a body that could not function. In the second case, God would give us the strength, day by day, to carry on with the struggle. I really did not know what was best, and it was so good to give it all over to Anne's Creator, who loves her even more than we did.

On Monday the 11th, Anne was still alive, but being kept alive artificially. Paul and I decided to go to the hospital together. Anne did not seem alive anymore. The effect of the curare and medication had left her completely motionless; she was unconscious. Only the wave movements of the monitor and the noise made by her respiratory machine bore witness that there was still life in this little body laid on the white sheet of the bed. Anne's eyelids were held shut by pieces of adhesive tape so that the light would not injure her eyes, as her eyelids were paralyzed as well. All of this seemed to help us become accustomed to the idea of Anne's imminent death. She already looked dead, and as soon as the tubes and cables were removed, everything would be over....

We took each other by the hand, approached the bed and prayed together in front of our child, who seemed to be drawing to the end of her brief passage with us. We did not usually pray so boldly, but that day, the ICU team's opinion of us was of little concern. We asked the Lord to free Anne from this situation, whether through death or through a miracle of His grace allowing her to breathe on her own.

Paul and I left hand in hand. Despite my immense desire not to leave my child for the last time, I understood how useless it was to stay at the side of my unconscious baby. We headed for home, our heads empty, and we mechanically took the subway, and then the car. At home, Matthieu demanded my full attention. My little boy, nearly three now, seemed to have completely forgotten he had a little sister. Perhaps it would be better for him if Anne's story ended now; Matthieu would have his mom with him every afternoon.

Boldness and Success

On Monday, January 12, Anne's death still hadn't come. I had to leave for work before authorized calling hours at the ICU. After dropping Matthieu off at the day care center, I went to a nearby Junior High school, where I began the medical examinations of the students.

My nursing assistant, Marie, asked me about Anne, as she always did. She immediately understood, that morning, that I did not have much hope left. I told her that I was waiting for a phone call from my husband at 9:35 am.

Marie made some coffee to comfort me. She and I began our work, which had become a routine. I had become quite incapable of taking any innovative initiatives. While examining healthy students, I asked myself questions: Would I hear of my daughter's death in this Junior High infirmary, with, as only source of comfort, a woman whom I barely knew? Would I then carry on with my routine until midday, as if nothing had happened?

At 9:30 am sharp, Paul anxiously called the hospital, and he spoke to Dr. Maurice who had been on call that night. Dr. Maurice said, "I tried to stop the curare and to lower the ventilation pressures during the night. It seemed to me that by moving the tube with my hand, I sometimes succeeded in obtaining satisfactory spontaneous breathing when the tube was left in certain positions. I then scrutinized Anne's file once again. Anne's condition worsened again during the night, with frequent episodes of respiratory arrest. At other times, I was able to make her breathe on her own by moving the tube in the trach opening."

Paul said nothing, wondering what point Dr. Maurice was making, why that morning he was explaining in detail his thoughts on the situation. He still had not said how Anne was doing! Dr. Maurice continued: "I became absolutely convinced, when I looked at the file from the beginning, that we had to replace her tracheotomy tube with a much longer one. I then remembered an improvised system I had once seen, a system with an intubation catheter that had been inserted through the tracheotomy orifice and was secured in place by a collar and a tightening screw placed around the tube."

He explained all of this calmly, still not saying whether Anne was still alive. Paul supposed so. Why would Dr. Maurice have given all these details only to announce Anne had died? But Dr. Maurice hadn't told Paul that Anne was doing better, either, and had actually said Anne had stopped breathing during the night, when he had attempted to stop the curare.

Dr. Maurice went on: "I contacted the ENT specialist on call that night to come and replace the trach tube. The ENT doctor refused, because the tracheotomy was too recent to be tampered with.

Because of Anne's clinical aggravation, I really had no choice, so I replaced the silver tube myself with a long plastic intubation catheter, which I inserted through her tracheotomy orifice. After going down about five centimeters, I met an obstacle. I was not sure whether or not I had reached the *carina*. I risked a perforation if I pushed further. But I risked this, attempting to go beyond that obstacle, thinking it might be a tracheal stricture, which could be the cause of her respiratory distress. I forcibly pushed the tube down beyond the obstacle. Anne immediately began to breathe spontaneously, and her color improved rapidly. Two minutes later, she smiled at me!"

Dr. Maurice went on, still with the same calm, unchanged voice: "She hasn't had any arrest since then, she's been breathing well, I unplugged the machine, and just left her on a little bit of oxygen, which she breathes in on her own. You can come see her... Anne's much better than yesterday, at least for now."

When Paul called me at the school, I was astounded at first, and then became firmly convinced that God had intervened. We had our miracle.

At last, someone had finally had the conviction, as I had, that Anne's tube did not cover the entire damaged segment of the trachea, someone had taken the responsibility of making the risky and controversial decision of inserting a long catheter, taking the risk of perforating the trachea.

Anne had smiled, Dr. Maurice had said! I remembered our prayer, the day before, by Anne's bed. Yes, indeed the Lord had intervened. Our Lord had used a man who himself had told us he did not believe in God, but who had the professional conscientiousness to scrutinize Anne's entire file, and had been convinced of what he had to do, alone, in the middle of the night.

As soon as I heard the news, I felt like going to the hospital immediately, but I also dreaded a new setback. I forced myself to go at the same time as usual. Matthieu needed my presence before his naptime. At 2:00 pm, I left home, leaving Matthieu to Paul, who had returned from work to take care of him.

At 3:00 pm, I entered the unit, my heart pounding. My anxiety forced me to always go to the bathroom before ringing at the door of the intensive care unit. As I came out, I met Dr. Péron himself. Even he, who seldom spoke to parents, leaving that responsibility to the doctor on call, couldn't help smiling and telling me, "It's amazing... you'll see! Dr. Maurice did the right thing at the right time!"

Strengthened by the immense hope of improvement, and not used to such enthusiasm coming from an ICU doctor, I rang at the door of the unit. A resident arrived immediately – it seemed they always came faster when there was good news! – and let me in, saying, "Dr Maurice took a great risk, and he won."

I quickly donned a sterile gown and went into the room. The difference from the day before was astounding. Today Anne was very much alive, when yesterday she had been at death's door! A smiling nurse accompanied me to the room. Anne was connected only to the monitor and the gastric tube. She was no longer paralyzed by curare, had no rectal catheter, no IV, nor were her eyelids taped shut. Most of all, she was rosy and conscious. She certainly did not look in perfect shape, but resembled a tired, ailing patient rather than a child on her deathbed. I immediately saw the special device used as a tracheotomy. The intubation catheter, a small, flexible plastic tube that looked like a drinking straw, came out of the trach opening at the neck and protruded about three centimeters from the skin. The catheter went down about six centimeters on the inside, and was secured by a screw fixed to a small collar attached with a lace behind the neck. Thus it was possible to safely move the small tube up and down as needed.

Dr. Maurice explained to me what he had already told Paul on the telephone. Dr. Maurice had been working for 24 hours straight. I thanked him profusely for his intervention. As if he wanted to minimize its importance, he said that the situation was certainly more comfortable now, but that the basic problem remained. I could nevertheless see the joy in his eyes, though he did not dare express it.

Dr. Maurice repeated his previous words on the phone, "As soon as I went beyond the obstacle, she smiled... it was amazing!" I felt tremendous gratitude toward this man! What would have happened if Dr. Maurice had not been there that night? He was the only one who had the courage to take this enormous risk despite the opposition of the ENT specialists.

Somewhat later, a doctor came into the room (I received many visits that day). She was also a Catholic Sister, a member of a religious order, and worked as an ICU physician. She told me, "I know that you prayed for Anne right here. Dr. Maurice told me so today when we saw the spectacular improvement together. He told me, half-jokingly, 'You see, the parents prayed yesterday... and the miracle happened!' "

How did Dr. Maurice know that we had prayed in the room, even though he had not yet arrived in the unit?

It is true that the miracle happened through the hands of Dr. Maurice. It is often when human solutions have been exhausted, when we think that everything is lost, that God takes over.

She Lives!

Were we now to believe that Anne was going to live after all? The doctors did not want us to get carried away after her January 12th miracle, and they had implied that Anne would probably experience further bronchospasms. But days went by, with neither spasms nor arrests. She was now breathing room air spontaneously, without machine or oxygen. Every day I marveled seeing her alive, conscious and often smiling. I spent longer periods of time with her. Now that she was no longer on the machine, I was able to take her in my arms again. I felt every little bit of progress was another victory over death.

At that time, a little baby named Sabine, who was about nine-months old, was extubated successfully. Sabine had suffered from paralysis of the diaphragm from birth, had been ventilated by a machine, and tracheotomized for several months. She had then been able to breathe without the machine, and eventually without the tube. Her parents visited rarely, but the nurses brought her into the hallway for a walk, all dressed up, giving us hope that one day, Anne would also walk in the hallway, dressed and without a tube! A few weeks later, Sabine was transferred to a regular pediatric unit. It was encouraging to see a child successfully discharged from Intensive Care.

On January 23, Anne still experienced no arrest. The miracle was continuing! Dr. Maurice had now taken her case to heart and he was the one making the important decisions. Since I had begun to speak with him everyday, I was much better informed of the situation. I became familiar with the machines and the ICU jargon used in reference to Anne. Since I had only her case to keep in mind, there were many questions and ideas that I could discuss with him each day.

Because I understood Anne's situation and obviously was personally involved, I became more active and useful. This enlivened me. It was so much easier for me, when I encountered a difficult or a painful situation, to be actively involved than to sit by passively and feel helpless!

Chapter 6
Special Attention

According to her chest X-ray, Anne's tube went down very deep, near the very end of the trachea. After a few days, Dr. Maurice decided to move it up about two centimeters, in order to see if it really was vital for it to be placed so deeply. He feared that the tube might irritate the tracheo-bronchial junction. Immediately, Anne began to experience difficulty, so Dr. Maurice decided to lower the tube. Once again he felt a resistance, which showed a lower *tracheal stenosis* (narrowing).

We realized that the position of the tube was crucial, right to the millimeter. If the collar loosened slightly, the tube slid up and Anne immediately breathed with difficulty.

Dr. Maurice had the nurses measure the length of the tube several times a day, to make sure that it was properly in place. Dr. Maurice posted the necessary distance in millimeters above the bed. The nurses were not accustomed to this practice, because the length of the tube for tracheotomized children usually did not matter a great deal.

I was afraid one of the nurses would not be cautious enough and Anne would suffer a respiratory arrest once more. After the great joy of her "resurrection," I began to worry again.

I realized that I was not fully at peace as this new preoccupation began to obsess me. Anne always seemed to look toward the window instead of looking at us. A horrible doubt began to arise in my mind. What if Anne could not see, or could only see the brightness of the window? What if we succeeded in saving her life, but she turned out to be blind? I had no logical basis for thinking this. I was simply afraid. I was afraid we would never have a healthy daughter, that there would always be something wrong with Anne. Complete healing seemed like such an impossible dream. Yet Anne was doing better! My feelings had been tried so often they no longer seemed to obey any logical reasoning.

I tried to make Anne follow my fingers with her eyes. She was five months old now and should have been able to follow the movement and turn her head. Instead, Anne continued to stare into space. My idea seemed absurd. Why would she be blind? This thought began to obsess me. One day, I awkwardly mentioned my fear to a nurse. "Oh," she said, "You're thinking that she might have after-effects from all the oxygen she received?"

How could I not have thought of that earlier? Highly concentrated oxygen is toxic for the optic nerve! Now I was really afraid. I was reassured somewhat, by the fact that the doctors had not said a word to me about that possibility, but perhaps they simply had not noticed! Until now, my worst fears had usually proved to be justified. How far was our ordeal to go?

While fearing the worst, I tried to stimulate Anne visually. I brought her colorful little toys and I made funny faces. One day, Claude, the nurse who was always so attentive, asked me if I wanted to give Anne a bath myself. What a gift she gave to me that day! I was, at last, going to do something useful for my child!

The nurse usually washed the children in the morning. Knowing that I arrived in the afternoon, Claude decided to wait for me so that we could give Anne her bath together. This gift was worth more to me than millions of dollars. Anne, stimulated by the bath and held in our arms, began to smile and look at me again. Claude explained to me that Anne's fixed stare had been a result of hospitalization syndrome, because she had been lying down for weeks without moving or seeing anything but the ceiling. I was quickly reassured that she had visual capacities. Claude's perceptiveness allowed me to take care of my child, make her more alert, and remove my anguish.

Now, when I arrived in the ICU, I had better things to do than just stay seated on a metal stool for three hours by Anne's bed. This daily bath became a real ceremony. I cherished these moments so much that I made them last as long as I could.

During these first days, Claude stayed with me to reassure me and show me what to do and how to do it. It was quite a process indeed. We would first stop the cardiac monitor and unplug the electrodes, then clamp the gastric feeding tube, and lastly remove Anne's wrist restraints. Now Anne was free from all encumbrances.

Anne did not, of course, look like just any baby taking a bath. A tube came out of her nose, another tube came out of her neck, and electrode wires adhered to her chest. But none of these were plugged in at bath time. She was absolutely free!

During the bath, we unplugged everything; no more monitor! I had to become accustomed to not seeing the monitor show Anne's cardio-respiratory rhythm. The very fact that Anne was moving in my arms was sufficient proof that her heart was beating, but I had been accustomed for weeks to live according to the monitor. Although temporary, it was a first step toward emancipation; a first step toward a new life.

Claude allowed me to give the bath entirely on my own. I did not resent the presence of a nurse, but I yearned so strongly for this intimate contact with Anne that I was overjoyed by the simple fact that I no longer had to rely entirely on the nurses to take care of her. I devoted about an hour to this ceremony. Anne became more awake and aware, and my afternoon was filled with sunshine.

I asked Anne-Marie, the ICU head nurse, if it would be possible to bring a musical mobile into Anne's room. Much to my surprise, she agreed, told us to bring it in and she would have it sterilized. From that time on, Anne had something other than the ceiling to look at while we were absent, and she heard Brahms' Lullaby thousands of times!

Better Days

Anne had two respiratory arrests on February 6, but Paul and I realized her tube had gone up a few millimeters. After it was put back exactly in place, everything returned to normal. It seemed the main bronchus was normal, since Anne had no respiratory arrests when her tube was properly placed in her trachea. My morale was better, and I began to hope she would survive. When I was away from the hospital, I still felt my anxiety, and I noticed I had lost nearly six kilograms (15 pounds) in three months. When I was with Anne, my anxiety decreased greatly, for she was alive before my very eyes.

Anne was going to be six months old on February 25. This seemed like a great victory to us, especially since her condition was stable enough when the tube was well placed. We wanted to celebrate this birthday, but not triumphantly, because we knew much could still happen. We also wanted to express our gratitude to the Intensive Care team who had helped Anne survive.

I asked Claude if it would be appropriate for me to give the team a birthday cake. She thought it was a great idea, and I had two magnificent cakes made in a bakery. Written on one of them was "Anne, six months;" on the other, "Thank You." On February 25, I left the cakes in the head nurse's office. Then I quickly went to see Anne, and gave her a long birthday bath! A nurse even took pictures, the first pictures taken of Anne in months. Anne offered us big

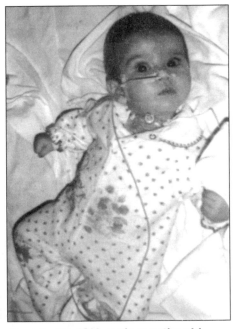

Anne in the ICU at six months old.

smiles for the occasion, as if she too were celebrating the fact that she had survived half a year!

Around 5:00 pm, the personnel gathered for the weekly staff meeting, followed by refreshments. Our cakes were, therefore, an appropriate addition to the program. Around 6:00 pm, a nurse came into the room and invited me to join the team. I hated to leave Anne, but was happy to be invited to the party.

The noisy crowd gathered in the small room intimidated me a little. Oddly, I felt like an outsider. I often participated in this kind of meeting during my medical studies, but today, I was, above all, Anne's mother, the mother of a child in the ICU. It became clear to me that day that the two roles could not be mixed.

Dr. Péron told me with a smile that he would open a bottle of champagne on the day Anne was extubated successfully. I was very happy to see Anne's future was now considered a possibility. I did not yet allow myself such long projections into the future, but I was overjoyed that Dr. Péron would do so. I answered half-jokingly, looking even further into the future, "And Anne will invite you to her wedding." Dr. Péron laughed and said he would be quite old by then! After this short venture into a still very uncertain future, I came back to reality. Taking advantage of the fact that no one was paying attention to me anymore, I sneaked out and went back to see Anne. I was glad I had thanked them for what they had done, but I belonged with my daughter.

Anne received two wonderful presents from the unit. First, the day after the party, the team gave her a larger tube, to facilitate her breathing and limit the dreaded risk of mucous plugs. Until then, her tracheal tube's internal diameter measured only three millimeters. The new one was 3.5 millimeters. This may not seem like much, but this increase made a very perceivable difference. The doctors made sure that the tube was carefully inserted down to the exact same length as the former one.

The next day, a second, more wonderful present was given to Anne: she was transferred to the "yellow section." The yellow sec-

tion was a real promotion for children in the Intensive Care unit. The
ICU was divided into three sections: the "red" and "blue" were sections of high intensive care, each with six IC rooms. Two nurses
were assigned to each section, one for three children, each child having an individual room. The yellow section was located in the back
of the unit, and included six rooms, to which fewer nurses were
assigned because the children there were in less critical condition.

Moving to the yellow section meant going from low odds of survival to somewhat higher ones, although children who left the yellow section for a pediatric ward sometimes never completely
recovered from their serious illnesses. Anne-Marie, the head nurse,
was delighted to move Anne into the yellow section. Anne had not
been on the ventilator for several weeks, and had a larger, more
secure tube. Both Anne-Marie and Claude had suggested this transfer to the doctors, who had agreed. Anne-Marie greeted me with a
large smile as I arrived on the 27th. "You'll see, we put her in a
sunny room, you'll like it." These few friendly words went straight
to my heart.

In the world outside the hospital, few things mattered to me. In the
hospital, on the other hand, everything was of tremendous importance – a thoughtful word brightened my day, an abrupt comment
could be greatly distressing. Before Anne's sickness, I thought I was
strong and not very emotional. Now, however, I realized that I was
emotionally vulnerable. Little by little, my hard shell of pride and
facade of strength built up over the years were crumbling. I was
learning the value of gentle words, the sweetness of friendship like
I'd been experiencing with Maria, the importance of God-given
compassion. I was learning to accept my weaknesses.

Each time I arrived in the ICU, I quickly walked all the way down
the hallway to the yellow section, without turning my head to the
right or the left, to avoid seeing children in the blue and red units. It
was not out of fear, rather out of respect for them and for their parents' need for privacy, and because I knew Anne risked returning
there if her condition worsened.

The children in the yellow section are not ventilated. They breathe on their own, differentiating them from the red and blue units. There is a marked difference in the atmosphere in the yellow section. You can hear the small premature infants cry, because they are not ventilated anymore. A few children are playing in their beds, and sometimes an older child will call a nurse. These life noises are reassuring. In the red and blue sections, silence is broken by the regular and monotonous noise of the machines working to preserve life.

During the long months spent in Intensive Care, I rarely knew anything about other hospitalized children, except for Chakib, whom we were happy to join in the yellow section. He had a tracheotomy, but lived rather peacefully, waiting to be old enough to be extubated. He was a lovely child, gaining weight, and his mother was hopeful his "trach" tube would soon be removed. She had been told to expect Chakib to need the trach tube three to six months, but she firmly believed it would be only three months.

Now that I knew how to unplug Anne without help, I took her with me to meet Maria and Chakib in the hallway of the yellow section. Because Anne and I were not allowed to stay in the hallway, she and I visited Chakib and his mother in his room. This was quite contrary to the hygienic rules of an intensive care unit. The nurses closed their eyes to this, knowing how good it was for us to see each other with our babies in our arms, like two friends meeting in a public park. At three and six months old, our babies ignored each other completely, but she and I jokingly said they were "pals," which gave them back some humanity which had been lost during their medical isolation. Maria and I often took the subway together after leaving the unit, and she and I discussed our impressions, as well as the changes that this experience with the Intensive Care Unit had produced in us. We could already see the positive aspects. In reality, we were administering mutual psychotherapy. Maria was very direct, and though she had no medical training, she was very quickly accepted by the ICU staff. She was not intimidated by the medical aura, and often, quite impertinently, gave her opinion on Chakib's situation.

The Others

Many children only stay in Intensive Care for a few days. They are transferred to a regular ward as soon as their condition becomes more stable. Others pass away quickly. All intensive care units have such cases, patients not stable enough to be transferred into a regular ward, but who continue to depend on certain life support services. Anne and Chakib had become "chronic patients."

I managed to get to know the other long-term hospitalized children, and the fact that they were in the same situation as my daughter automatically made me sympathetic toward them. I was told that there were four "chronics" in the unit. There were two boys and two girls, including Anne.

Sabine was the little girl that the nurses liked to walk around in the hallway. Because she was doing better and had been extubated, she had been moved out to a pediatric unit.

One of the little boys died after a few months. Prior to this, I had met his mother in the change room and had exchanged a few words of sympathy and understanding with her. One day, we found ourselves in the same subway car, as we were both heading for the hospital. I discovered that this young woman, who was barely twenty years old, had to leave her husband in another region of France, and had been living with an aunt in the Paris region for a few months, so she could come see her child who had been on a ventilator since birth. That day, she was happy because he had recently begun to breathe without the machine, although he still needed a high oxygen concentration. I had just turned 30 myself and was struck by the fact that such a young woman had to mature so quickly, and go through such an ordeal so soon after her adolescence. She told me she feared her son might be deaf. My heart went out to her. I'd had similar fears about Anne just a few weeks earlier.

One day we arrived together at the entrance of the change room. When we rang the doorbell, a nurse rushed to the door. It was not something they usually did, and I was immediately worried. I was relieved it was not about Anne but I feared for the young woman.

The nurse told her a doctor was going to talk to her before she went in. I entered quickly, not wanting to eavesdrop. I went directly to the yellow section, looking straight ahead. That evening, as I left, I avoided looking in the little boy's room. I asked no questions.

The next day, I prayed for this young woman I'd just met. I never saw her again. I soon realized there was another child in his room. It was unthinkable that his condition might have improved spectacularly enough to justify transferring to another unit. I knew that he had died. A nurse confirmed this a few days later.

The Lord had taken him. Why him and not Anne? Why now? Why not earlier? I believe this tragedy is somehow included in God's sovereign plan. I do not understand His plan:

> *"Oh, the depth of the riches of the wisdom and knowledge of God! How unsearchable His judgments, and His paths beyond tracing out! Who has known the mind of the Lord? Or who has been His counselor? Who has ever given to God, that God should repay him?* [1]

After the departure of Sabine to another service and the passing of the little boy, Anne and Chakib were the only two "chronics" left.

Anne and Chakib

Chakib was always dressed very nicely. Maria explained to me that she had brought his own clothes. I happily did the same thing for Anne. Of course, the electrode wires were a bit bothersome, and I had to make a few small holes in her clothes so the wires could go through, but these were easily surmountable details, and I finally knew the joy of dressing my little girl. I was thrilled to buy clothes for Anne when I shopped. It was tangible proof that she was alive!

---

[1] Romans 11:33-36.

Chakib and Anne were assigned the same ENT specialist to care for their tracheotomies. Maria firmly believed in the rapid healing of her son and was looking forward to going back to Casablanca soon. As for me, I did not allow myself to think about Anne's discharge from the hospital. I was simply happy she was alive, and the idea of her departure seemed completely unreal to me.

Just as Maria had predicted, Chakib was extubated at the beginning of March. The first attempt was successful, and a few days later, Chakib left in excellent condition.

That day, the nurses dedicated their full attention to Chakib. He had been there three months, and everyone was quite fond of him. He was one of the victories of the ICU. Chakib was actually leaving for home, not just to another unit of the hospital. He displayed no after-effects after three months of intensive care. This was rare enough to justify a celebration. One after another, the nurses went to his room, directly opposite ours, to say goodbye, write down his address, and give him a little gift.

I suddenly realized children left the ICU in good health. It was happening right there, before my eyes. This gave me hope, but also made me realize how tired I was. Until now, Anne's struggle between life and death had dominated everything. Her struggle was no longer all-consuming. We were alone, facing the long, uncertain future, a true test of our patience. How long would Anne stay here? During the first few months of Anne's hospitalization, I didn't allow myself to consider this question. Long hospitalization meant survival, and that was what mattered most.

Chakib's departure, as Anne's condition was becoming less critical, gave us hope. I was, of course, aware that Anne's and Chakib's cases could not be compared. One day, a nurse was comparing Anne and Chakib. A doctor immediately put an end to her comparison with the words: "It's completely different for her...." Indeed, Chakib's ailment was well-known, and the doctors knew the odds of survival were high if the patient was treated well.

Anne's situation was quite different. Her respiratory malformations were almost unique. The few similar cases published in the worldwide medical literature usually had a fatal outcome. I supposed that Anne, like Chakib, would only leave intensive care once extubated. How many months would be necessary for her trachea to be firm enough to no longer need a stent? Would that ever happen?

On the day of Chakib's discharge, I was deep in these discouraging thoughts, giving Anne a lengthy bath to fight my boredom, Claude thought of me in a wonderful way, which I will never forget. After having said goodbye to Chakib, Claude came into our room and told me, "It must be hard for you, but you'll see, one day it'll be Anne." Only Claude had thought of saying something like this. Yes, it was difficult for me, but after these few words of consolation, I felt better.

Maria also came to say goodbye. She wanted to believe Anne would soon go back home: "I will only be perfectly happy when Anne is extubated and at home," Maria told me. This was so kind of her. We promised each other we would write and see each other again whenever Maria came back to Paris. "When Anne is well," she said, "you'll come visit us in Casablanca. We also have a vacation home on the Mediterranean, near Ceuta."

"Why not," I told myself! I can dream!

We each kept a picture taken by a nurse of the two children together in our arms. It would be a good memory. Who knew if we would ever see each other again? We had experienced many intense moments together, surprisingly forging an unusual spiritual sisterhood for two women from such different backgrounds and cultures.

Chakib left the unit in excellent condition, Anne was the only chronic patient in the ICU. She became the faithful mascot of the unit.

More Autonomy

Following Chakib's departure, Claude encouraged me by teaching me to suction Anne's tracheotomy tube. Anne had to be suctioned every hour, day and night, to remove secretions that had accumulated in her tracheotomy tube.

Sometimes, when I was with Anne, I could tell she was very congested, but I did not dare disturb a nurse who was working in another room. This congestion often provoked coughing and vomiting. Anne still vomited often and was not gaining weight. She had nice plump cheeks that looked very good, but her thighs and her buttocks were quite skinny! Perhaps I would be able to prevent her from vomiting if I suctioned her in time?

The act of tracheal suctioning is simple, but it needs to become automatic if it is to be performed correctly. During suctioning, Anne's tube was almost completely plugged, which affected her breathing. The process has to be brief, but also long enough or repeated enough times to be effective. My ear had to become acquainted with both Anne's normal and abnormal sounds, to the various gurgling, snoring and whistling noises. A humid congestion is not dangerous, but a dry one can be fatal.

I learned how far down to go with the suctioning tube – low enough to be effective, but not so low the trachea would be damaged. I was on the lookout for bloody mucous plugs, which could clog up the tube by forming clots. I developed the reflex to suction every time Anne vomited, so she wouldn't inhale her stomach contents.

It took time to acquire these skills, but they were essential to Anne's survival. Claude taught me. Other nurses also helped me and encouraged me. Still others did not appreciate this new freedom I'd been given. Fortunately, I did not see them much, because I rarely needed their assistance.

When Anne vomited, I changed her sheets and clothes myself. Just before leaving, I plugged in the monitor and feeding tube, reattached her wrist restraints to the bars of the bed. All that was left to do was to notify the nurse. The nurse was often busy in another room, and it was more convenient to plug everything back in, than to wait for the nurse. At this time, I only saw the short-term interest of this independence. It helped me combat boredom by giving me something to do. I no longer had to depend on the nurses to care for Anne. Neither Claude nor I suspected, at that time, how useful this information would be later.

Alerts

On March 18, the medical team attempted to move the tube up two centimeters (a little less than one inch). More than two months had gone by since Dr. Maurice's life-saving intervention, and we were hoping that the *tracheal stenosis* had widened due to the pressure of the tube. The results were rather favorable during the first hours, and the doctors considered leaving the tube in this position for about ten days before completely removing it.

The next day, however, we realized that Anne was not doing well with the higher position, and the tube was reintroduced to its initial length. Was there absolutely no progress? Would we never succeed in extubating her, in getting her out of intensive care? Anne had been there four months by now and the outcome was not clear at all. Chakib had left as a healthy baby, but Anne seemed to make no progress whatsoever.

At Easter, Anne's situation worsened. I had felt reassured, until then, by the fact that, when her tube was in the proper position, the risk of her death was kept at arm's length. Yet when we came to see her on April 14, Anne was breathing with difficulty and looking gray, which was frightening. I immediately checked the position of the tube. The tube was at its normal length. What was happening? I was very worried.

I had the ICU physician on call paged. He was not a regular member of the unit, and, not knowing Anne well, did not seem too worried by her condition. I shared my worries with him: "Anne isn't well, she worries me." He did not seem convinced. "She hasn't given us any problems today," he said.

Not yet, I thought.... But were we going to wait for a serious problem before doing something? I did not want to leave Anne's room without at least encouraging the ICU physician to be especially cautious that night.

"Usually," I told him, "she's like this when her tube slides up too far."

I showed him the small sign put up by Dr. Maurice, indicating the height of the tube in millimeters. He took a ruler and measured it. "It's at the right length," he announced.

Of course, I thought, as if I did not know that! "That is precisely what is worrying me," I added. "Until now, we've always solved this kind of difficulty by sliding the tube back down to its normal height."

He did not really know what to answer. "I'll keep an eye on her tonight. For now, she doesn't worry me," he said.

What else could I say? He was not worried, but I surely was! I had no solution to this new problem. Very late that evening, I left the unit reluctantly. If allowed, I would have stayed all night.

My heart was full of fear. "Lord," I prayed, "Please watch over her! I am leaving but you are staying! Show the doctor what to do if she stops breathing!"

At 9:30 am, I called the ICU. Dr. Péron answered. "Anne had a major respiratory arrest at 7:30 this morning. She is better now. You may come whenever you wish."

"Even this morning?" I asked.

"Come now, if you want," he said.

Paul and I immediately left for the hospital, fearing the worst. We knew what "arrest" meant in intensive care terms: It is a cardio-respiratory stoppage leading to death if it lasts too long.

Upon our arrival, we saw the resident to whom I had spoken the previous day. He had just finished his shift and looked exhausted. He explained: "Anne wasn't doing badly during the night, then suddenly, she had an arrest at 7:30 am This is the worst time to have an arrest. The night personnel are ready to leave, and everyone is waiting for the day team to arrive. Anne had a long respiratory arrest, which triggered *bradycardia*, necessitating external cardiac massage and ventilation with a mask for ten minutes. The cerebral anoxia led to a loss of consciousness and a seizure, indicating cerebral distress. She frightened me greatly. I remembered, at that point, what you had said about the length of the tube, and I decided to push it down five millimeters. There was immediate improvement."

He concluded by saying: "Fortunately, you spoke to me about this yesterday evening, and it came back to me suddenly, at the most critical moment."

I thanked the Lord for answering my prayer. We entered Anne's room. She was breathing calmly, sitting propped-up, half-asleep because of the Valium administered to stop the seizure. Dr. Péron was in her room and smiled warmly. He said, "The first EEG, done right after the seizure was abnormal. We did a second one two hours later and it was normal. There is no brain damage."

Sabine

I was both relieved and frightened by Dr. Péron's announcement. In a flash, I recalled all of the arrests Anne had experienced. I realized that with each arrest, Anne could have sustained irreversible brain damage. I hadn't considered the possibility of caring for a living, but mentally handicapped child!

Paul and I had lived in the fear of death, but not of brain damage. Yet, as a physician, I knew that inadequate oxygen to the brain leaves irreversible damage if it lasts longer than three minutes. Why hadn't I ever thought of this? At any rate, it was probably better that I hadn't.

When Anne awoke, we took her in our arms and saw that she had lost none of her responsiveness and vivacity! Together, Paul and I thanked God for protecting Anne's brain that morning, and also for all the other times when we did not realize this great danger.

We had no explanation for this arrest, apart from the possibility of the tube being too short to cover the area of stenosis. Yet the tube had remained at the same length. There were, therefore, two possible explanations: Either Anne's trachea had grown and required a longer tube, or the damaged area was extending down lower, toward the main bronchus.

This second hypothesis was of serious concern. From then on, the doctors began to speak of *bronchotracheomalacia*, [2] thinking the damage was not limited to the trachea, but extended to the main bronchus. I mulled these thoughts over and over in my mind. After three months of respite, would we have a new setback because of the extension of the damage? The risk of Anne's death loomed before us once again.

Anne was now seven months old, and we again risked losing her at any moment. That morning had almost brought the end, or even worse, she could have been given back to us alive, but brain-dead. Yes, risk of death and the danger of brain damage were still present. Perhaps I had already come to take her life for granted. This episode reminded me of the frightening reality that *life is but a breath.*

"...What is your life? You are a mist that appears for a little while and then vanishes." [3]

A few days later, on Easter day, we saw a striking example of what could have happened. Sabine, the little girl who had been extubated and sent to the pediatric unit in good health, came back to the ICU. We did not know it immediately, because no one spoke about the conditions of the other children. After walking by her bedroom

---

[2] Bronchotracheomalacia — flaccidity of the trachea and the main bronchus.

[3] James 4:14.

several days in a row to reach Anne's bedroom in the yellow section, I recognized her. I did not stop. I thought that she had probably been brought back because of a setback in her respiratory condition. Soon she was transferred to the yellow section, just opposite Anne's bedroom. Thinking she was doing better, I told the nurse: "Sabine is in the yellow section, it seems she's doing better now! I'm glad!"

I could see from the look on her face that she did not share my joy. "She's not doing so great," she said simply.

I then noticed Sabine was sitting in a baby chair and she seemed to be breathing well, but was not playing with the toys that were hung in front of her, even though she was now one year old.

The next day, I asked the nurse: "Is Sabine not doing well? Did she become sick in the pediatric unit?"

"She became congested," the nurse told me. "Then she had an arrest. When they transferred her here, it was too late. We were able to save her heart, but that's it!"

And so Sabine, the first "chronic" to be extubated, the example we hoped to follow, had suffered brain damage. She lay there, listless, in her baby chair. What would become of her? Her parents rarely came, even when she had been doing well. I had not seen them since her return to the ICU. She died a few weeks later. I felt sincere sadness. She was at an age where she should have learned to stand and take her first steps. Would Sabine have made it if she had received better care outside the ICU? I was almost certain of it. I felt angry toward her parents who appeared to have abandoned her. Perhaps they could have warned the pediatric service of this respiratory congestion if they had been there. I felt angry toward the pediatric unit that apparently had acted too late.

I promised myself never to allow Anne to be transferred to a pediatric unit. She would either stay here or go home, where I could constantly watch over her. I trusted no one. I promised myself to always remain vigilant, to stay with Anne each time I felt that her life was in danger, even if that meant spending the night on an iron stool and standing up to the opposition of the medical personnel!

This determination, acquired that very day, proved very useful to me. No nurse, no doctor, no matter what position they occupied in the medical hierarchy, intimidated me anymore. I knew they all had their shortcomings, and I had to be the most vigilant of all, for Anne was my daughter. This attitude was not always well received, particularly in some hospitals where the staff did not know us; but for me, there was no doubt I would stay with Anne anytime I felt she was in danger. I noticed that the best-qualified and most trustworthy personnel didn't mind my presence and even encouraged it.

In the ICU, I learned, little by little, to perform all of the nursing tasks for Anne. The doctors always talked to me before making an important decision. Dr. Maurice told me one day: "You always end up being right anyway!" It was friendly sarcasm, but there was some truth to it, for I had only one child to care for!

The end of April went by with no major problems. The tube was positioned deeper and Anne was breathing well. She was still vomiting often, became congested easily, and was not gaining much weight, but was part of our daily lives. The beginning of May arrived, and there was no solution in sight. We were not going to leave her in intensive care for the rest of her life, yet as soon as the tube was brought up a millimeter or two, Anne was in danger of another respiratory arrest. We were in a very uncomfortable situation.

It was far too dangerous to remove her from the Intensive Care Unit and put her in a normal pediatric ward. That would have been out of the question. None of us, including Paul and I, wanted to take that risk. Anne had been here six months! I remembered the little boy whose mother I befriended just before his death. I thought about Sabine, who had suffered brain damage and then died. Do intensive care "chronic patients" stay for months, only to pass away? Was there absolutely no hope! Yes, there was! Chakib had gone home healed!

I would not give in to despair! Chakib was now a normal child, and his hospitalization belonged in the past. I wanted to believe Anne would one day be able to live outside of an ICU. After all, I told myself, she had lived in good health for three months before being hospitalized. If it was possible before, it should also be possible afterwards.

I had posted a few pictures of Anne "before" in her bedroom and that boosted my morale. I also remembered the dream I had before her first hospitalization, a dream that had inspired patience in me rather than discouragement. A friend of ours, Pastor Collins, also encouraged us: "I believe that she will live and will be an example of God's grace." Because these words came from the mouth of a man of prayer, a man who did not speak without thinking, a man who did not take lightly his commitment to the Lord, they touched us very much. Yes, God was powerful enough to overcome seemingly hopeless situations. Anne had not died when we expected it most and were ready to face it. God knew the solution, and His timing for Anne's situation was perfect!

Chapter 7
Attempts

The ICU physicians were perplexed. To test Anne's progress, they placed the tube one centimeter higher. Anne went rapidly into respiratory distress and they had to lower the tube, once again forcing their way down through an obstacle. What should they do with a child who was doing well, but whose life was in danger when the trach tube slid up a millimeter?

The doctors thought this blockage could be a *granuloma*, a sort of overgrown wing of the trachea caused by the trach tube. If this were true, they could treat the *granuloma* and solve the problem. Once again we had hope. On May 6, Dr. Tristan, an ENT specialist, performed a bronchoscopy under general anesthesia. There was no *granuloma* but rather a narrowing of the lower third of the trachea. Our hopes of treatment blew away with the wind! Unable to improve Anne's condition during the bronchoscopy, Dr. Tristan advised a total extubation a few days later.

We were surprised! How could Anne tolerate breathing without the trach tube if she could not even tolerate it being a few millimeters higher? It seemed illogical, but we were at a complete dead end. It seemed worth a try.

On May 10, the catheter was removed completely. The procedure, which took only a moment, seemed so simple! Much to our great joy and surprise, her condition did not worsen significantly, as it had in January. She even seemed better than when the doctors had tried to slide the catheter up. We dared to be hopeful and even began to imagine her out of the hospital. After all, Chakib had left the hospital three days after his extubation.

Anne might be home in a few days! If she did well the first few hours, why not for a longer time? For the sake of security, we would leave her in the hospital for a little while, but she might leave on May 18, Paul's birthday! I was excited about that possibility. Paul had done so much these past six months to help me through this ordeal. What a wonderful birthday present!

I watched Anne very closely, the entire afternoon. The hours went by so slowly! If only we could reach twenty-four hours without the tube! As the hours ticked by, it was becoming increasingly difficult for her to breathe. She became agitated and cried in my arms.

It was a joy to hear her cry, since the catheter had kept her from uttering the slightest sound. I would have preferred to hear her laugh or chatter, but the sound of her crying was music to my ears. I had not heard anything like this for months! For a few hours, we had also removed the gastric tube used to feed her. What a joy it was for me to see this small face with no tube or tape and her neck with no collar or screw! I felt as if in a dream. It had all been so simple.

I tried to give Anne a bottle with milk, but she became even more agitated and refused to drink. Yet, to leave the hospital, she had to eat without a gastric tube! Because she had not been fed normally for such a long time, she seemed to have lost the swallowing reflex.

What worried me the most, though, was her increasingly noisy breathing. She sounded like a small steam engine climbing a hill. When evening came, I could not leave her. She was too agitated to go to sleep. I cradled her in my arms, pacing around the room. She finally went to sleep, only to wake up suddenly as soon as I tried to lay her down on her bed.

Beyond the physical fatigue, I also felt the mental fatigue created by this mixture of great hope and anxiety. If I sat down just one moment to rest, she started to cry again. She quieted down only when I cradled her. I was tired of pacing around the room. But Anne had to remain calm, so she would not waste her breath crying.

I saw a nurse pass by and asked her if she would replace the stool with a chair, so I could rock Anne, hoping that it would keep her calm. I could finally sit down. Anne went to sleep, but her breathing remained difficult and noisy. As I rocked her, balancing on the back legs of the chair, I sang songs of praise to God. This calmed us both.

The ICU physician on call often walked by the room, glanced in for a second, but did not come in. I wondered if my presence kept them from intervening. If that were the case, it would have been better for me to leave; however, I refused to leave Anne in such a precarious condition and go home. If I left, I would always wonder if I should have stayed.

If they wished to suction or decongest her, couldn't they do it in my presence or ask me to leave the room for a few minutes? The dilemma was cruel. If I left her, they might act more freely and more efficiently. On the other hand, her condition could worsen dangerously, without anyone by her side to notice it immediately. Things could happen so fast! I promised myself once again never to leave Anne while she was in such an unstable condition.

For one moment, the doctor stopped at the door of the room, as if hesitating to come in. I immediately seized the opportunity to share my concern with him, "She isn't doing too well. She's making a lot of noise." He nodded without saying anything, then walked away. How I wished Dr. Maurice were there!

I had now been alone with Anne for about ten hours. Her condition was worsening gradually, and no one came to check on her, much less to talk to me. How I longed to communicate with someone! Since I was afraid of leaving Anne, even for only a moment, I had not eaten anything since that morning. I was not hungry, but I was exhausted.

At 11:00 pm, Anne's shortness of breath worsened once again. This awakened her. Anne was exhausting herself like a child suffering from an acute asthma attack. I was hoping that she would soon be reintubated. A nurse came in, and together we tried to clamp and suction her, with no real improvement.

The minutes dragged by. Anne could no longer sleep. At midnight, the doctor decided to reintubate her. Would he have waited longer if I had not been there? Was he yielding to the temptation of giving rest to both mother and child? It had become obvious in any case, that Anne would not have been able to hold on much longer. She risked a serious arrest at any moment. Even in this highly competent medical unit, I would not have left Anne, as the watchfulness of the most qualified personnel could not compare to that of a mother living in quasi-physical communion with her child.

The doctor decided to reintubate her through the nose instead of using the tracheotomy opening, which, after a few hours, had begun to close. I left the room during this procedure, which requires much calm and technical skill, especially with Anne in respiratory distress. I was perfectly willing to leave the room, not because I could not bear to watch such a procedure, but so that I would not disturb him. I was determined to see, understand and participate as much as I could, so that I could be as helpful as possible in the treatment of my daughter's illness. I paced in the hallway for a few minutes. The doctor came to join me: "It went smoothly," he said. "Anne is doing much better."

Anne was calm and rosy-colored. The bronchial congestion had been easily suctioned as soon as the tube was inserted, and her breathing was no longer noisy. What a marvel that small plastic tube was! I felt great relief, yet all plans of bringing Anne home had vanished. Exhausted, she went to sleep immediately. I put her in bed, connected her to the monitor, and, reassured, returned home in the early morning hours.

Upon reflection, the experience had not been an entirely negative one. Anne had breathed without the tube for about 12 hours, while she had tolerated extubation for only 15 minutes on the previous attempt. The team decided to make another attempt on May 18, this time leaving a suction tube in the trach opening to suction the secretions.

May 18 – new hope! The first hours went remarkably well. After the relative failure of the previous experience, we did not really dare to hope! However, when Dr. Péron saw Anne smiling and playing in her bed after four hours without a tube, he could not resist a little optimism, "Perhaps we'll be able to open the champagne soon."

The evening arrived slowly. The minutes and hours were unending. I wanted Anne to go beyond the 12-hour mark already achieved. I was hoping the inflammation would diminish, since the tube was no longer irritating the mucous tissues. Then, miraculously, we reached the 12-hour period! Anne's condition deteriorated, but less than before. That night, she went to sleep rather easily.

Anne made it through the night! It was a victory! She wasn't doing as well as during the first hours. When I arrived at the hospital, I found her very short of breath, but not critical.

I had hoped to claim victory after the second day. What a mistake! For six days, Anne remained very precarious, constantly short of breath, tired and hardly ever playing. To ease her breathing, she was kept sitting. The air humidifier was replaced by an oxygen humidifier. She was still being fed by gastric tube and vomited almost everything. She remained conscious nevertheless, was quite a rosy color, and her blood gases were not too bad. We had to continue. Perhaps she would turn the corner and begin to improve.

How long would this last? How could she go home in this unstable condition, constantly on the verge of an arrest! Was it better for her to breathe poorly without a tube, or to breathe well, but intubated? This was the first time I asked myself that question. Could I bring Anne home while constantly breathing with difficulty? How many months, how many years would she suffer?

I had the misconception that an extubated child immediately lives a normal life after seeing Chakib. How naive I was! These six days were among the most difficult in my life. I stayed by Anne's side late into the night, leaving reluctantly, fearing that something might occur.

I had a constant headache from the tension. I had trouble eating and lost more weight. Despite all the anxiety, I held onto the hope Anne would come back home and the comforting certainty that:

"...in all things God works for the good of those who love Him, who have been called according to His purpose." [1]

At home, I did my best to take care of Matthieu, whom I only saw between 12:00 and 2.00 pm, as I continued working every morning to retain my medical benefits. [2] I prayed daily that he would not suffer too much from my absence.

God answered my prayer through the friendship of Jean-François, a five-year old boy who adopted Matthieu as a little brother. This friendship was a blessing, because Matthieu had always been a loner and this new relationship helped develop his personality. Jean-François' mother, a friendly neighbor, frequently invited Matthieu to their home.

I always hurried on my way to the hospital, not wanting to miss a single minute with Anne, and anxious to know her condition. As soon as I would see the red building, my eyes were riveted to the fourth floor, looking for a sign of comfort which, of course, I did not find: the windows always remained closed.

Each day I raced up the stairway to the fourth floor, except on the rare days when the old elevator was working. I arrived at the entrance of the ICU, out of breath, always feeling a short instant of hesitation: Was I able to accept today's reality?

On May 20, I rang at the entry of the unit. "Come in!" they motioned. This meant Anne was there and she was still alive! I went straight to her room. She was sitting in a baby chair, breathing with difficulty. Since the extubation, I did not dare take her away from her oxygen aerosol, and, therefore rarely held her in my arms.

I was glad Claude was working the dayshift again, and was able to spend time with us. She helped me cope with this new ordeal. This

---

[1] Romans 8:28.
[2] Employed by an American missionary organization, Paul did not have access to French national health insurance, whereas the children and I received full benefits through my job, provided I worked a minimum number of hours.

time it was different. I felt we were inflicting this trial upon Anne. All we had to do for Anne to feel better was to put the tube back in place. I kept asking myself, "Is this really worth it? What can we hope for? How long is this going to last?" To persevere meant to keep hoping Anne would improve enough to come back home.

As I arrived on May 25, I found Anne sitting as usual in the baby chair, the humidifier dispensing its usual oxygen flow. She was breathing with difficulty, but not moving. She was unconscious. A quick look at the monitor revealed *tachycardia* (fast heart rate), showing a cardiac reaction to the situation, but not *brachycardia* (slow heart rate), which could soon occur, if a critical lack of oxygen to the heart and brain was reached. I glanced around rapidly; there was no nurse in the yellow section. It was the time when Claude left for lunch, leaving her tasks, as was usually done, to a nurse working in the blue section. Claude knew that I always arrived around 3:00 pm and Anne would not be alone for a long time. Everything went very fast. I went into the hallway and beckoned to the ICU physician who hurried to Anne's room, followed a few moments later by Claude, informed of the situation by a colleague in the lunchroom. Few words were exchanged, but the appropriate gestures were eloquent. Anne was reintubated within less than two minutes and regained consciousness. That was the end of this nerve-wracking experiment, which had lasted seven seemingly unending days and nights.

Claude was distraught and felt very guilty that she had left Anne for a few minutes. She was extremely embarrassed I had discovered my own daughter unconscious in her room. I was too aware of the precariousness of Anne's condition to consider Claude guilty of anything. I knew that a nurse could not stay with her eyes riveted on my daughter all day. As a matter of fact, the monitor would have given the alert a few moments later. Nevertheless, I could once again thank the Lord for placing me in the right place at the right time.

As soon as she was intubated, Anne's skin regained its healthy colors and her body began to function well again. What a delight to see her play and smile once again, after such a struggle!

Chapter 8

Some Research

After this series of failures, it seemed unreasonable to consider another extubation. On the other hand, how many more months were we to leave Anne in Intensive Care? At nine months of age, she needed to get out of bed, to play, to learn to stand up. And Matthieu needed me at home!

No one at the hospital seemed to have a solution. A tracheal transplant, which was still experimental, seemed out of the question. We were facing a dead end again. Then I read, once again, the following verse:

> *"Trust in the Lord with all your heart, and lean not on your own understanding; in all your ways acknowledge Him, and He will make your paths straight."* [1]

I asked God to give me the wisdom of a solution. The doctors were just as helpless as I was in regard to Anne's condition.

Half a day each week, I went to the medical school library (where I had worked on my doctoral thesis) [2] to research all the publications that pertained more or less closely to Anne's case.

Within a few weeks, I was able to compile nearly fifty articles. I only found two cases in worldwide medical literature that closely resembled Anne's case. These two children – one Russian and the other American – had right *pulmonary agenesis* [3] as well as *tracheomalacia.*

---

[1] Proverbs 3:5-6.
[2] In France, medical doctoral programs, like other doctorates, require the elaboration of a doctoral dissertation.
[3] Right pulmonary agenesis – Failure of the right lung to develop, absence of the right lung.

The Russian child had never been intubated. His tracheal anomaly was probably less critical than Anne's. The child suffered from a very precarious respiratory condition. Numerous bronchial infections had created damage in his only lung. I preferred Anne's situation. The tube, which allowed for suctioning, provided protection for her lung.

The American child had been intubated at the age of three months. His case was almost identical to Anne's. At the age of nine months, after repeated extubation failures, a surgical procedure had been chosen; resection-anastomosis of the lower trachea and the beginning of the main bronchus. [4] This was exactly what should be done for Anne.

The results of the procedure interested me greatly! The American child's surgery had gone well, but infection complications required additional surgery on the main bronchus. The child deteriorated considerably after the second operation, and he died a few days afterwards. This confirmed the ICU physicians' concern; it was necessary to be cautious, especially considering that Anne was doing well with her trach tube.

I discovered another interesting case. A Canadian child had two lungs, but severe *tracheomalacia*. The medical team used the same system of a long tube mounted on a collar with a screw, in order to stent the flaccidity of the lower trachea. Like Anne, the child had done poorly with the attempts to slide the tube up. He was finally extubated at the age of three without surgical intervention. This encouraged us to be patient and cautious.

On June 1st, the doctors tried to extubate Anne again. This time, she rapidly developed tracheo-bronchial infection. Her condition became serious within just a few hours. Refusing to leave, I stayed all night. My presence was not really permitted. I dared not ask for

---

[4]   A procedure basically entailing the cutting out of the damaged portion of the trachea and main bronchus, and suturing the healthy parts together.

permission to stay for the night, as it was against the rules. I simply stayed, as discreetly as I could, and no one sent me out.

Around 5:00 am, it became necessary to reintubate Anne. Hope was brief once again!

June was a mixture of uncertainties and unexpected progress. We were uncertain as to the strategy we should adopt. Since the first extubation attempts in May, Anne had been intubated through the nose. The tracheostomy hole had closed. Should we open the tracheostomy again and use it for an extended period of time before attempting anything else or should we keep the nasal intubation, knowing it was less comfortable and threatened to eventually damage the vocal cords, but permitted repeated extubation attempts?

We decided to keep the nasal tube for another month and then to attempt one last extubation. Anne would receive cortisone. There was much at stake.

Revolutions and Progress

Developmentally, Anne's progress was remarkable. Two things revolutionized her life in June 1980. First of all, following Paul's initiative, we were allowed to bring a walker into Anne's room. Paul, with his delightful naivete, succeeded in many of his requests from the ICU. Anne was the star of the ICU for them to allow such liberty!

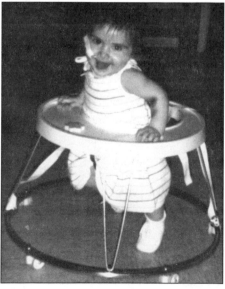

Indeed, Anne was becoming very mobile thanks to her walker. She pulled on

Anne in walker in the ICU at 10 months old.

the electric plugs and medical tubes in her room, and soon undertook racing through the room and the hallway of the yellow section.

At first, the walker was only used when Paul or I were there to supervise her. But little by little, the nurses became quite fond of this small vehicle that brought a little bit of amusement to the unit. When they had a bit of free time in the morning, they would put Anne in her walker and watch over her as she raced down the hallway. They unplugged her gastric tube and folded it into her clothes so that she would not run over it! Anne's development made a great leap forward. Her environment was no longer limited to her bed!

The second great and unexpected joy of the month was even more surprising. One lovely June day, a nurse suggested we take Anne out in the hospital gardens for a few minutes! I was speechless! We were in an intensive care unit where children lived in complete isolation in sterilized rooms and not even grandparents could visit. And we were talking about taking a stroll in the garden!

I shared my great surprise with the nurse. "It has happened once or twice in the history of this unit," she said. "Ask the ICU doctor about it." Much to my surprise, he agreed with a smile. "Don't go too far," he said. "And don't stay too long!"

I could not believe my ears. Anne was about to go out of the ICU for the first time in nearly eight months! At a time when a permanent discharge seemed less likely than ever because of the extubation failures, it would be a great breath of air and freedom for all of us.

What a joy to walk with her beyond the doors of the ICU, which separates the

Paul with Matthieu and Anne in the hospital garden – Summer 1982.

world of healthy people from that of the critically ill! Not knowing where to put Anne while I was changing, I went down to the garden wearing the gown, hat and slippers of the ICU! We only stayed outside for a few minutes. She still needed to be suctioned frequently, and we could not take her away from her humidifier for long. But what joy to share this news with Paul as soon as he arrived at the hospital!

We began to go outside every afternoon, June being warm and sunny. This new reality changed our life considerably. Matthieu was finally able to see his little sister. We were thrilled to be reunited after seven months of separation and finally be a family once again!

There was a beautiful willow tree in the garden, which gave us shade on very hot days and a wonderful background for family pictures. This scene looked like an impressionist painting, only a small cafe on a river bank was missing from the portrait. This was our summer holiday! We were just as happy as many families who vacationed far from their homes. Do not the greatest joys often come after the greatest trials?

On May 25, we celebrated Anne's ten months of life – each month of life was a victory. Anne could now receive a limited number of visits. My 80-year-old grandmother, like the rest of our family, had lost hope of ever seeing Anne alive again. It was a moment of great happiness for her, and a moment of great emotion for us, when she took Anne in her arms.

Going outdoors, as well as using the walker inside, had truly stimulated Anne's development. Only the tubes coming out of her nostrils showed that she was a hospitalized child. Her energy and enthusiasm gave a falsely reassuring impression, and those who saw her outdoors wondered what she was doing in Intensive Care. We, however, knew only too well her life depended on a small tube 3.5 millimeters in diameter, placed in its proper position, and suctioned regularly to avoid becoming plugged.

Last Attempt

July 1st finally arrived. Anne was medicated with steroids and sedatives, preparatory to a last-chance extubation. We all knew what was at stake; in case of failure, Anne would need a long-term tracheotomy. We all hoped for success. The ICU doctor on call knew Anne's case well and kept her under close observation. He gave her oxygen so she would not tire quickly, and had her clamped and suctioned to avoid tracheobronchial infection. Unfortunately, these efforts did not stop Anne's condition from gravely deteriorating. The blood gases became dangerously abnormal. Greatly disappointed, the doctor had no choice but to reinsert the tube after less than twelve hours!

We were discouraged, which was understandable. We knew we had to trust in Anne's Creator. This ordeal was long and we could not see the end of the tunnel, but despite our impatience, we knew Someone saw and guided her life.

At that time, I wrote the following short text in my journal to reflect my thoughts after so many human failures:

> *"When we know God, it is easier to wait, knowing that He controls our circumstances and that our ordeals are not the fruit of blind fate. When the trial becomes unbearable, He is there to bear it in our place; He carries our burden, His peace replaces the anguish in our hearts.*
>
> *When things go better, it is usually we who are less faithful and try to understand and act on our own, which only creates yet other sources of worry. Numerous verses in the Bible were written by or for suffering people. We all have the same weaknesses and our faith is small despite the example of previous generations.*

It is comforting to see that King David himself felt the same anguish as I, or that John the Baptist also had moments of doubt concerning Jesus. We do not understand God's ways, especially in the heart of trials: 'Who can understand His ways?' (Romans 11:33)

Thank you, Lord, for walking before me to open the way and walk with me in through this long ordeal, whose end I cannot see. I feel as though I were climbing a mountain, watching for the mountaintop at each switchback, surrounded by dangers as I ascend, always hoping the next turn will be the last and no danger will touch me there, but this road always climbs higher and further....

Yet one day I will reach the top and I will be able to look back and see that You have accompanied me the whole way. Thank You, Lord, for Your Word which encourages me, for your Holy Spirit which fills me. Do not let me quench the work of the Spirit because of my unbelief."

On July 8th, Anne was tracheotomized once again. It took us a while to get accustomed to seeing her breathe through her neck and the nasal tube again, but, on the other hand, her face was now free from the tape and the tube; only the small gastric tube remained. The steroids had made her look a bit plump, but had been discontinued. Anne looked much prettier now!

Many doctors and nurses had left for their summer vacations. Paris was emptying itself of its inhabitants, as it did every summer. Several people expressed their regret that we could not leave on vacation. This surprised me, for I hadn't the slightest desire to go anywhere! I was happy when Anne was doing well, unhappy when she was not. Everything else mattered little to me.

Of course, the value of a child's life cannot be compared to a trip to the beach. But was it possible for others to really understand our situation?

The subway was filled with tourists, conveying a holiday aura. My job in school medicine had stopped during the summer vacation, and I was therefore able to devote my mornings to Matthieu. Paul got up very early, worked until two in the afternoon, then took charge of Matthieu so I could go to the hospital. At six o'clock, both came by subway to join me at the hospital.

Often, when the weather was good, Paul and Matthieu would leave earlier so we could have a family time on the hospital lawn. I then returned home with Matthieu, while Paul stayed with Anne until she went to sleep around 10:00 pm, then took the subway home. How much longer would this kind of life go on? Months? Years?

Yet we were not unhappy. We lived one day at a time. Each day brought a new blessing; some progress by Anne, a good time spent with Matthieu. At the same time, how we would have liked to live together, all four of us at home! One day, as we were talking about it, we realized that if this happened someday, we would know a happiness that few families know. We thanked the Lord in advance, assured of this promise in God's Word:

> *"Let us not become weary in doing good, for at the proper time we will reap a harvest, if we do not give up."* [5]

Intensive Care Closes!

As the summer went by, we could only wait, with no medical solution in sight. We were discouraged. Then, the Lord acted in an astonishing and unpredictable way, far beyond what we asked for in our prayers.

One day, Anne-Marie, the head nurse, told me the Intensive Care Unit would close in September for cleaning and renovation.

What a shock! I had never conceived of an ICU closing.

---

[5] Galatians 6:9.

I felt as if I had been betrayed; they couldn't do this! What would they do with Anne? Were they going to endanger her life just to repaint the walls? Anne was the last "chronic" patient in the ICU. Other children were to be transferred to other ICU's, premature babies to neonatal units and the Saint-Gilles ICU would stop admitting patients a few days before closing. It seemed Anne would be transferred to another ICU in Paris.

No one liked the idea. Her case was so unusual, she had been at the Saint-Gilles ICU for such a long time and her survival was so astounding, no one wanted to put her in anyone else's hands. Moreover, she was now so alert and healthy-looking when her tube was well positioned that she did not seem to belong in the world of intensive care.

We had six weeks to find a solution and none of the options seemed satisfactory.

On July 23rd, Matthieu left for Brittany [6] to stay with his grandparents. This gave more time to find a solution. Anne was scheduled for a bronchoscopy on July 29th. We hoped that its results would be encouraging and would allow the ICU to attempt an extubation in August. Anne would then be one year old. Perhaps her trachea would have grown sufficiently to allow the air and the secretions to pass easily through the affected area.

For this bronchoscopy, Anne was transferred to St. Xavier hospital where the ENT specialist Dr. Tristan worked. Accustomed to the stringent security and hygiene of intensive care, I was shocked by the general state of this ENT ward. The beds nearly touched each other in small, shabby rooms. Many children were left completely to themselves, waiting to be operated on or having just returned from the operating room.

No humidifier, no ventilator and no suction machine were installed for Anne's bronchoscopy. A nurse's aid came every now

---

[6] Brittany – La Bretagne, French province located on the NW Atlantic coast.

and then, glancing around the room then leaving. If I had not come, who would have watched over Anne, who was still under 24/7 cardio-respiratory monitoring? What about the risk of contamination from children with runny ears and noses all around her?

Once again, I was very glad that I had come. I obtained a bottle of normal saline solution, instilling a few drops in her tube every now and then to compensate for the lack of humidity in this over-heated room.

An hour later, Anne was taken to the operating room for the bronchoscopy. This procedure could last as little as ten minutes or as much as two hours. Would she then go to the recovery area or return to the overcrowded ward?

The only means to get news of Anne's bronchoscopy was to stay by the door of the operating room, to catch Dr. Tristan as he walked out. He would not, I thought, come to find me in Anne's room. In fact, he did not even know that I was at the hospital. There were no seats in the hallway, no waiting area anywhere near the operating room. I just paced in front of the door.

Why was there no waiting room where surgeons could come to see parents after an operation on their child? Why was it often necessary to be pushy to obtain information? Was she not my child? Do surgeons only see parents as a bothersome hindrance?

It is not only material conditions but also a profound change of attitude that is necessary. Parents need to be properly greeted and informed, they have the right to understand and ask questions about their child's situation.

I tried to pray but was not able to concentrate. I then remembered with gratitude, the following verse from the Bible:

> *"...the Spirit helps us in our weakness. We do not know what we ought to pray, but the Spirit himself intercedes for us with groans that words cannot express."* [7]

---

[7] Romans 8:26.

My prayer was an inarticulate groan of anxiety, but God's Spirit "translated" it in my behalf to God the Father. The same passage continues:

"And He who searches our hearts knows the mind of the Spirit, because the Spirit intercedes for the believers in accordance with God's will." [8]

Even though my thoughts were completely confused, I knew God had a clear idea of the situation.

Dr. Tristan came out an hour later. I immediately walked toward him with the uncomfortable impression of overstepping my bounds. Dr. Tristan was a very friendly man, but always in a hurry, and never seemed to have more than five minutes to give. He was probably already late for another appointment, yet I had to talk to him, and it is a good thing I did, because this conversation changed our life.

At first, the news seemed to be very discouraging. Dr. Tristan drew a small sketch to show that Anne's trachea was very much reduced in width over the lower 15 millimeters and the main bronchus also seemed to be strictured (narrowed). In short, Anne could not possibly live without her tube.

"But," I asked, "for how long?"

He looked at me gravely. "It's severe *tracheomalacia*. It can last months, even years."

"But," I asked, trying to stay calm and minimize the importance of this information, "will she have to keep a tracheotomy tube for several years?"

"It's likely," he answered. And, as if to alleviate the bad news, he went on. "Tracheotomies are well tolerated by children. In this ward, we have tracheotomized ten-year-olds who are doing well."

---

[8] Romans 8:27.

Was this supposed to be comforting? Was he insinuating Anne might keep her tracheotomy until she was ten? Or was he helping me realize she might need one for the rest of her life? When I was a medical student doing a clerkship in ENT, I had observed school-age children with tracheotomies since birth, and virtually lived at the hospital. It had never come to my mind this might be Anne's case.

The compression of the main bronchus was worrisome as well. Would we have to once again go through the anguish of a major operation to remove this compression? Dr. Tristan did not seem to think so: "I often see this condition on the main bronchus of children. It may not amount to anything. I'm not in favor of an operation in her case. The risks are high and the outcome very uncertain."

"My Ways Are Not Your Ways"

In just a few seconds, these revelations changed the future of our family for years. Until now, we calculated in weeks and months. Month by month, we waited for the trachea to have grown enough to function without artificial support. Now the ENT specialist was speaking of years! I then remembered the article on the Canadian child extubated at three years of age. I also recalled Dr. Koop's letter, telling us that a long-term tracheotomy would be the best solution. He also had spoken of a waiting period of three or four years.

A new idea suddenly came to me, and I gathered my last ounce of courage to question this specialist, already halfway out the door.

"If this situation lasts five to ten years, will Anne have to stay at the hospital the entire time?"

I expected a vague answer, but I was astonished to hear him say, "No, I don't think it would be absolutely necessary for her to stay in the hospital. Some children with tracheotomies are treated at home...."

With that, he left.

I had heard enough. Anne was going to go home with her tracheotomy! I had never really considered this possibility before, nor had anyone spoken to me about it. All our efforts had been focused on extubation, which seemed to be the indispensable pre-condition for Anne's return home.

Anne breathed well when her tube was properly positioned. I had learned these past months to give her the necessary care. So, why not? I realized the ICU doctors might not share Dr. Tristan's opinion. They knew her so well, had saved her so often, and they knew what a fragile balance we had reached. Would they accept Anne's return home?

From that point on, I lifted up fervent prayers to God to allow this return. It seemed so unexpected, too wonderful to be possible.

We tend to have such a wrong idea of God! He is a Father, why would He not give us what our heart desires, if it is in accordance with His will?

> *"Which of you, if his son asks for bread, will give him a stone? Or if he asks for a fish, will give him a snake? If you then, though you are evil, know how to give good gifts to your children, how much more will your father in heaven give good gifts to those who ask him!"* [9]

This new idea absorbed my thoughts completely, opened up new horizons. For the first time in eight months, I was making plans! Still, I was not completely confident. Every day, as I arrived in front of the red brick building, I experienced the same moment of anxiety: Was Anne still alive? Did she have a future?

I had noticed that she needed walking shoes for her walker. Dare I buy some for her? Good shoes for this age were expensive. I caught myself wondering if such an expense was justified for a baby without a future. Not that I was expecting her to die, but she and I had been living for so many months in the present, not in the future.

---

[9]   Matthew 7:9-11.

Buying shoes seemed like a wager on the future I had no right to make. I even feared acquiring objects for her that could become relics if she were to die.

These first walking shoes seemed full of symbolism. They represent the child walking towards the future, discovering life, being more independent. Was I going to be terribly disappointed?

I tried to organize my thoughts rationally. Anne needed shoes now. She ran everywhere in her walker, barefoot. I was not going to

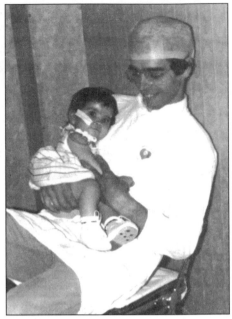

Paul holding Anne in the ICU at ten months, wearing her new shoes.

deprive her of what she needed because of some sort of complicated masochism.

Satisfied with my reasoning, I went with great pleasure to a pharmacy to look at walking shoes for babies. I wanted to tell the pharmacist: "You know, this is quite an occasion! It's for my little girl who is almost one, and has been in the hospital all her life! She's going to walk, she's going to live, she's going to run towards the future!" But of course I said nothing of the kind. To say these things would have mixed my two worlds, revealed my intense relation with Anne, with the hospital personnel, with those who could understand, even with God. I was not yet ready to mix these two realms. I simply chose a pair of shoes, paid and hurried out, shoebox under my arm, to the hospital. This purchase was not part of a dream, or some whim. Anne would wear her shoes in the hospital today! As for the future, God would take care of it. He was only delegating to me the responsibility of the present.

I was even more fearful that day than usual as I arrived at the hospital, as if making an investment in the future would compromise that future. I realized my fears were superstitious. Such fear does not come from God. He loves us and protects us, and does not allow us to undergo trial for no purpose. God is love!

> *"There is no fear in love. But perfect love drives out fear..."* [10]

---

[10] I John 4:18.

Chapter 9

Teamwork

My firm plan now was to bring Anne home before the closure of the Intensive Care Unit on September 1. This gave us a month to get organized. Having obtained the ENT specialist's implicit approval, I just knew I could persuade the other doctors. I was motivated! Yet the ENT could not make this decision, being only a consulting specialist, not Anne's principal physician.

In Intensive Care, my task was to convince three doctors: Dr. Péron, the ICU director, and his two assistants, Drs. Maurice and Houlette, who cared for Anne on a daily basis. Dr. Péron received Paul and me in his office and warned us of the dangers. First of all, there were physical dangers: Would we know how to act rapidly if a mucous plug formed in the tube? Did we realize how much medical equipment we would need? But he also insisted on the psychological risks of such a decision: "It will be a very anguishing situation for the whole family. Think about your son, your marriage. We would not want to be responsible for a divorce!"

We listened without objecting, but as long as he did not give us a categorical refusal, our minds were made up. Of course, the situation would not be easy, but we were convinced that our marriage would hold, for

"...A cord of three strands is not quickly broken." [1]

Paul and I formed two strands, the Lord was the third that consolidated the whole.

Moreover, our marriage had already been strongly tested for several months, and I felt strongly convinced that this situation would

---

[1] Ecclesiastes 4:12.

be easier for me than to leave Matthieu and Paul every day for five to six hours. Would we be able to withstand the pressure of being fully responsible for her survival? We did not know, but we were ready to try. I was now well-trained, thanks to Claude who had taught me all the necessary techniques: physiotherapy, suctioning, changing the gastric tube, etc. If she had not been there to teach me, I would not even consider bringing Anne back home!

Dr. Péron finally told us he was not against this experiment, provided that we be in constant contact with an ICU sufficiently informed of Anne's condition. Dr. Maurice, who had been following Anne's case directly, gave his approval, as did Dr. Houlette. All of them made it clear that this was an exceptional experiment. It would be best to take Anne home a few days before the closure of the unit, in order to bring Anne back if we were unsuccessful, in which case she would be transferred to another Paris ICU.

Preparing For the Big Day

I suggested a departure date to the doctors. On August 25, Anne would be one year old. Returning home would be a wonderful birthday present for our little girl!

Everyone in the unit helped us prepare. It was not simple. First of all, we needed a good bit of medical equipment. Certain machines, such as the monitor used for Anne during the night, could neither be rented nor reimbursed by health insurance. We also had to find a humidifier, a suctioning machine, and a whole list of paraphernalia such as gastric tubes, tracheotomy tubes, suctioning catheters, collars, tightening screws, wrist restrainers and so forth. We would need a liquid nutrient for feeding via the gastric tube, and three large bottles for daily disinfection of the suctioning catheters. The humidifier consumed more than a quart of distilled water per day. We would also need enough electrodes to change them daily, but these could not be found in pharmacies, as their availability is limited to hospitals.

Apart from these material problems, we had to be ready to take care of our daughter 24 hours a day by ourselves: Suctioning her trachea every hour, day and night; feeding her through her gastric tube; recording details of our care, hour after hour. We also needed to write down hourly the nature of the secretions, copious or not, clean or dirty, thick or fluid. We had to record the amounts she was fed and vomited, as well as the daily quantities of urine and stool. We regularly recorded her weight, respiratory and cardiac frequency rates.

All of this required much time, but was not too difficult. On the other hand, I did not feel quite as confident about emergencies.

"A mucous plug is always possible," Dr. Houlette told me, "and in those conditions, you can quickly lose the child. If this happens in your home, it will be dreadful, but you must not feel guilty about it. It can happen anywhere, even with the best care. Prepare for the worst, and take all the necessary intensive care equipment. The most important item is the prevention of plugs by humidification."

Claude prepared little cards to pin above Anne's bed telling us exactly what to do in different emergency cases. It was crucial to know how to recognize the different respiratory noises that signaled danger. The noise from simple congestion can be frightening, but not immediately dangerous. On the other hand, even a slight whistling sound indicates a tracheo-bronchial obstruction, whether created by a plug, by displacement of the tube, or by tracheal swelling. It is then necessary to act immediately.

Claude showed me how to regularly instill normal saline in the tube to avoid the formation of mucous plugs. Anne's catheter was only 3.5 millimeters in diameter. Such a small tube can be clogged up by mucous secretions that dry on contact with air. They become like gum glued to the walls of the trachea and, little by little, obstruct the air flow. This risk was even greater in Anne's case, because her tube was much longer than normal tracheotomy tubes. The plugs were formed little by little at the lower extremity of the tube, where the suctioning catheters were not very effective because of the curving shape of the trachea toward the lung.

It was essential for us to recognize if the obstruction was due to a plug, tracheal swelling (caused by an infection, for example), or to a bronchial spasm linked to the *tracheomalacia*. One can only differentiate between them by recognizing the sound, and the distinction is not easy to make. This is especially difficult in an emergency where one must act within minutes or even seconds to save a child who has ceased breathing.

Claude, Anne-Marie and Dr. Maurice taught me how to act quickly and to resuscitate Anne. Dr. Maurice deemed it indispensable that I know how to change the tracheotomy catheter. Indeed, in the case of a large plug inside the tube that cannot be eliminated, the only solution is to remove the whole tube, hoping the plug is inside the tube and not in the lower trachea or main bronchus.

Anne's case was very different from other tracheotomized children. Each person caring for Anne would have to become very familiar with her respiratory sounds, thus drastically limiting the number of people able to help us. It would be out of the question to hire a nurse for one evening and go to the movies! Only a well-trained person could be trusted to care for Anne.

This person needed to be able to change the tube quickly in case of an emergency and resuscitate Anne if she went into acute respiratory distress. To call a doctor, or even an ICU ambulance would probably be useless, as time is so short when respiratory arrest occurs. Moreover, the intervening emergency team would not know Anne's case and risk pushing the plug even lower in the trachea by attempting artificial respiration on a clogged tube.

We were going to have to be self-reliant, depending on our own resources. This would also mean that one of us would always have to be on call. In certain cases of emergency and fatigue, it would probably stretch us to our very limits.

Only God's help and presence allowed us to prepare for the future with confidence as we recalled that:

"I can do all things through Christ who strengthens me"
and *"...when you are [tested], [2] He will also provide a*
way out so that you can stand up under it." [3]

We were going to make these promises our own, one at a time.

Paul was now learning to suction Anne. He did not know how to insert a tracheotomy tube, this was indeed a very delicate technique, but in an emergency, he must at least know how to remove a clogged tube.

I was so strongly determined to bring Anne home that the awareness of the risks and the time required to care for her could not change my determination. I now had one overriding objective; to bring our daughter back home. For this, I was ready to mobilize all my energy!

Dr. Maurice prepared a kit containing products that could be injected or instilled into the trachea in case of cardiac arrest. He warned me: "If you need to use these, you will be in a nearly hopeless situation. If you can't get the child to breathe, it is virtually impossible to try to make the heart beat again."

How would we hold up physically if we had to wake up every hour of the night? Here, at the ICU, teams rotated every 12 hours, and then were off duty for half of the week. At home, we would have to take care of Anne 24 hours a day, 7 days a week!

Paul, moreover, worked during the day, and I would care for Matthieu at home. We would need help for the nights. The ideal solution seemed to be to have Anne under a home care arrangement with trained nurses coming regularly.

It seemed logical that home care would be accepted easily by the national health administration, being six times less expensive than the ICU. No home care service, however, was willing to take Anne's

---

[2] "Tested" and "tempted" can be translated the same from the original Greek.

[3] Philippians 4:13, I Corinthians 10:13.

case. The risk of death was too great, the case too difficult to manage. This was a great blow to us. We had prepared so well, and now everything seemed to be up in the air again. Would the doctors still agree to discharge Anne to us if no home care was available? Despite our great desire to have her at home, would we be able to live under such conditions with no help, barely sleeping, always on our guard? I was so convinced that God was in control that I knew we would find a solution. I spoke to Claude about it.

She was as determined as I to see Anne leave before the closure of the ICU. She told me: "For several nights now, I've been allowing more time between the tracheal suctionings. Once every three hours at night is enough, unless there is infection. If you take turns getting up, this makes only once every six hours for each of you. This is possible, of course, if Anne is put on the monitor while you're sleeping."

What a great leap toward autonomy! Once again, it was Claude who helped us over this hurdle that could otherwise have prevented Anne's discharge.

The big day was approaching. I still had trouble believing it would really happen. I feared that some last-minute medical complication would force us to change our plans. As for the practical complications, however, I had no doubt we would overcome them. But I feared that Anne's condition might seriously deteriorate before August 25, something that we could not control.

Having been refused by Home Care, we now had to obtain all the necessary medical equipment by our own means. I thus spent my mornings making telephone calls and establishing contacts and continued to spend my afternoons with Anne at the hospital.

I was able to rent a humidifier, an oxygen bottle for emergencies, and a suctioning machine. One problem remained; Anne needed a monitor to give proper surveillance during the night, allowing us to sleep between suctionings. We inquired everywhere and found it impossible to rent a monitor. To purchase one would cost thousands of dollars and would not be reimbursed by health insurance. With no other solution in sight, Dr. Maurice decided to loan us an extra ICU monitor. This expression of trust helped make up for the disappointment of Home Care's refusal.

The ICU physicians suggested that a few nurses accompany us to our home to set up everything. Claude, Anne-Marie and Christine immediately volunteered to come. I was so thankful for their thoughtfulness! Matthieu had returned from his grandparents' home in Brittany. We were going to welcome Anne as a family! The hospital routine had become so ingrained that bringing her home seemed all the more unreal.

The solidarity of the medical personnel and our friends was an immense help to us. Elisabeth, a Christian friend who was a nurse in intensive care at a University Hospital in Normandy, called to say she would take several days off to come help us. We would soon witness her competence, kindness, and faith in God, a real encouragement for surmounting the first obstacles and discouragements.

Going Home

Wednesday, August 25 arrived. The weather was good, not too hot; ideal conditions for Anne's discharge.

We arrived at the hospital around 10:00 am. On the large white board in Anne's room where daily medical instructions were ordinarily written, an inscription in bold letters immediately caught my attention:

DISCHARGE: 11:30-12:00

Magical words written on the wall! I took a picture of this inscription, as we wanted always to remember this great moment. Above these words, a sheet of paper had been prepared for us, including telephone numbers of ICU ambulances, and names of doctors to contact in other Paris ICUs.

Anne looked lovely, in a purple dress and white shoes. She of course did not realize how momentous this event was. Intensive Care

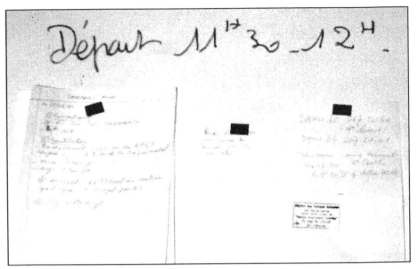

Anne's departure announcement from the ICU and instructions to take home – August 24, 1982.

had been her whole life. She was about to move to a strange new world where no one wore white coats.

The ambulance was scheduled to arrive at 11:00. Anne came out of her room in her walker as usual and was escorted to the ICU entrance by the nurses and doctors who said goodbye to her. Everyone stopped to kiss her, saying, "So, this is your big day!" and other such kind words. As we arrived in the entrance hallway, we saw Anne-Marie approaching with a large, colored bag. She knelt down and opened it before Anne's eyes. It was full of birthday presents given by the nurses and doctors.

In my excitement, I had almost forgotten that today was her birthday. I hadn't expected anything like this! The team had been thoughtful enough to buy a huge teddy bear for Matthieu, delighted not to have been left out of the celebration.

The ambulance arrived and this historic moment in our lives actually took place. After 264 consecutive daily visits to the ICU, each day anxiously wondering if our daughter was still alive, we were now exiting the ICU. Now she was with us, and we could observe her condition at every moment.

Until now, 18 hours of every day were spent without access to information on Anne's condition. For me, this daily uncertainty was the most difficult part of our long ordeal. Though we could call to receive news, we couldn't call every single hour! Yet I constantly needed to know how she was doing! The most reassuring words could not replace Anne's presence!

I made the trip home in the ambulance with Anne. The others followed in their cars. Even the ambulance attendants were caught up in the general excitement, as they asked me all sorts of questions about Anne, which I gladly answered. That day, I was full of good will toward everybody!

We arrived at our house and the ambulance left quickly afterward. We were at home and Anne was staying! I was then filled with a sense of great vulnerability! We had just cut the umbilical cord with the ICU team that had kept Anne alive for nine months. Would we be able to take over from here? Had we been too optimistic about our capabilities?

Departure day from the ICU – August 25, 1982. Left to right: Agnès with Anne, ambulance assistant, Claude, Christine, Anne-Marie.

Fortunately, the presence of the nurses reassured me, helped me to make that step. We were not yet completely alone; qualified and competent friends were surrounding us for a few hours.

I had prepared a birthday meal in advance, and we shared it with everyone. Anne was the queen, enthroned at one end of the table. She seemed not the least bit surprised by all this excitement. For the occasion and the pictures, we had taken out her gastric tube, but she could not yet eat through her mouth.

We would have to teach her to eat and drink. I knew, having already tried, that it would not be easy. She could neither eat her birthday cake nor, of course, blow out the single candle with her trach tube. This did not prevent us from sharing our joy with this team of nurses, who, from that day on, also became our friends.

After the birthday meal, the four nurses accompanied us for a walk around the neighborhood. Anne was in a stroller for the first time in her life. So many new things for her to experience all at once! Every now and then, folks would glance our way, guessing that this was the little girl who had been in the hospital for such a long time. I was proud to show off my daughter, but at the same time, I felt possessive, for she was finally ours, after months of being "on loan" to the hospital.

Weaning Us from the Hospital

Strong bonds had been forged between us and Anne's caregivers. I was so very grateful toward these people who had helped us save our daughter. I felt a profound attachment to them, which, understandably, they could not reciprocate, for Anne was not their child. We were also going to have to learn to live without the emotional comfort of their daily presence.

At first, I needed to call Claude daily. Then I began to realize my dependency had gone beyond the medical realm. We had forged a very close relationship with Anne-Marie and Claude, going beyond purely professional contact. It was both wonderful and complex to experience!

Claude and her husband Pierre came to our home several times. Pierre and Paul also got along well, which strengthened our friendship. I sensed a strange thing happening, something I neither liked nor understood; I felt comfortable only with those directly connected with Anne's case, those who had cared for her and were still doing so.

I was always happy to see doctors and nurses from ICU or to welcome Anne's physiotherapists, but was easily irritated when other people visited us, even old friends or friends from church who had prayed faithfully for us.

Unconsciously, I wanted to share our happiness only with those who had also shared our distress, who had experienced Anne's critical condition. This was unfair. My energy had been so entirely focused on my daughter's physical condition that I closed myself to everything else. Anne's care not only took my physical energy, I also felt emotionally dependent on everything and everyone linked to Anne.

A neighbor made a remark that hurt because it seemed unfair, but it also opened my eyes: "Your daughter seems to be the only thing that matters in the world..." she said, irritated after I told her that I was unavailable for some social activity. This refusal may have been necessary for Anne's security, but I had to learn to open up to the world again, to be interested in people who had no direct relationship to her. I became very troubled by this problem, and shared it with a close friend. She encouraged me to count, once again, on the Lord who had accompanied me during these long months of anxiety. She reminded me I could talk to Him about this problem without fearing to disturb Him; that I could ask Him to help me be more interested in the people surrounding me. I had to readjust to the normal world.

I followed her advice, and consequently decided to let Claude call me if she wanted some news, instead of calling her myself.

It took me several months to reach emotional independence, to regain balance in my life.

We remained friends with Pierre and Claude, but on a more normal, detached, less emotional basis.

I had the impression that people could not really understand what we had been going through, and the dangers we were still facing. I did not want to forget this and enter a world of pretense, to live as if nothing had happened.

In any case, the daily difficulties of having Anne home did not allow me to forget. In the neighbors' minds, Anne was back home, her life was no longer threatened. We knew that this was not the case, that the ordeal would be long, the outcome uncertain, the danger of an accident was still great. We had to learn to live in an unstable world.

Chapter 10
Hospital At Home

Our nurse friends left, after giving us countless bits of advice.

The first moments of euphoria had passed. The challenge of caring for a handicapped child in our home had begun. Thankfully, Elisabeth, our friend from Normandy, had come to stay for a few days.

Our first objective was to remove Anne's gastric tube. This small tube was very bothersome and uncomfortable and there now was no medical reason for Anne not to be fed normally. This was a vicious circle, because as long as she was fed through that tube, she was not hungry, and this hindered her from learning to eat.

Elisabeth and I decided to remove the feeding tube once and for all. We hoped that she would feel hunger and drink from a bottle or eat applesauce with a spoon. It was a trying experience. Anne refused to take the bottle or any other kind of food for 24 hours. She even refused water, risking dehydration.

After about 20 hours, the situation became alarming. Anne laid on her bed, without getting up or playing. She was exhausted. We had to reinsert the gastric tube and feed her through it once again. Her hunger seemed to make no difference. She would let herself die of thirst and hunger if we could not teach her to enjoy the experience of food.

Elisabeth had to return to Normandy. I had to continue trying alone! Anne desperately needed to gain weight, so I gave her high-calorie formula through her gastric tube. This formula had a good, sweet vanilla taste and I tried one last time to give her some in a bottle, but to no avail. She bit on the nipple, but as soon as she felt the liquid enter her mouth, she made a face and let go of the bottle. She also continued to vomit her feedings regularly.

During the evening feeding, Anne would go to sleep, become congested, begin to cough; then she would suddenly throw up the whole feeding in the bed, even though she still slept in a sitting position. It was then necessary to suction her trachea, because there was a risk of inhaling the feed. Then we needed to clean her, change her, change the sheets, start another feeding and pray that it would not happen again.

While Anne did well putting up with this ordeal, I grew more and more impatient and nervous, until one night, when I was at the end of my rope. I gave this concern to the Lord. It would be His problem now, not mine. Of course, I would still have to change the sheets, but whether she vomited or not was no longer my burden alone.

Every night for months, my prayer by Anne's bed came down to these three points: "Lord, help Anne to breathe well, to keep her food down, and to gain weight." Little by little, I learned to practice patience and daily trust in God. Anne continued to vomit regularly over a long period of time, but my attitude had changed. God was working in me and was "sculpting" me through the daily challenges that I faced. An immediate answer to my prayer would not have accomplished the same result.

While giving her a bath a few days later, I saw her sucking the water-soaked washcloth. She seemed to feel a sort of pleasure doing so, and was even swallowing a bit of water. Despite the obvious hygienic problems linked to such a learning experience, I encouraged her with many bravos and words of congratulations.

In a very original and personal way, she was learning again the lost oral pleasure, preferring water and soap to vanilla dessert! I did not dare push things by giving her water in a bottle, fearing she might reject trying to learn to eat.

A few days later, I used a small nipple with a tiny hole that would let the water (without the soap!) flow very gently. On August 30th, she drank 20 milliliters of water from the bottle. It was a beginning. Little by little, she accepted sugared water from the bottle in very small quantities.

This gave me the idea to make the transition between tube feedings and normal feedings by giving her a bottle every hour. She thus consumed about ten tiny meals per day. It was likely that her stomach, after nine months of tube feeding, would not take greater quantities at a time.

At the end of each day, I counted the calories that she had taken in. Ten days after her departure from the hospital, after all these efforts, we removed the gastric feeding tube; one less tube! Of course, Anne did not yet consume large quantities, but she now accepted high-calorie formula from the bottle and took in between 500 and 1,000 calories per day. On September 9th, she weighed 16 pounds... still not much for a one-year old child!

Return to Intensive Care

Soon we faced additional difficult events. Only three days after Anne left Intensive Care, her breathing became more laborious and wheezy. We had to suction her more frequently, even during the night. It appeared that something was plugging the catheter. We were worried. Paul and I were concerned and exhausted.

On Sunday, August 29th, friends from out of town came to rejoice with us about Anne's homecoming. They were extremely concerned about Anne, who was vomiting, wheezing and gasping. What should have been a day of celebration became fraught with worry.

After they left, Paul and I began taking turns checking on Anne during the night. In the morning, she was still breathing with difficulty and we had to take her to Intensive Care, two days before the ICU closed.

This return was very disappointing, but we were too preoccupied by the immediate situation to see it as a lasting failure. We were greeted with warmth and sympathy. The medical team decided to slide the tracheotomy tube slightly downward, and a control X-ray showed that the tube had reached the lower extremity of the trachea. Once again, two millimeters had changed everything! Claude was on duty that day, and immediately took charge of Anne. What a relief for me, after those tense and sleepless days and nights, to put her in Claude's loving and competent hands!

Dr. Houlette came to see me and gently explained that I would not be able to carry on if I slept neither day nor night. We had to find a solution.

"For tonight," he said, "I advise you to go home and rest. We'll keep Anne here. After that, it's essential that you find help for the nights. We've been in contact with the leadership of the Home Care administration so that they'll make an exception and take you on service, which would mean you would have help for the nights."

He convinced me. I was incapable of arguing with him in my fatigued state and was convinced he was right. We returned home leaving Anne in the hospital, only six days after her triumphal discharge, and one day before the month-long closure of the ICU.

Solidarity

Paul and I phoned friends and they formed a prayer chain. There were only 24 hours before the ICU closed. All our friends prayed for a solution. We did not want Anne transferred to another ICU merely because we could not meet the challenge physically.

We really felt the support of our Christian brothers and sisters. They prayed that the situation with Home Care would be resolved. When we returned to the ICU the next day, we were told that Home Care had made an exception and agreed to take us. We could bring Anne back home, and the Saint-Gilles Hospital Intensive Care Unit could close!

We began a night watch system with Sylvie and Thierry, two Home Care employees. Both were competent and reliable, and, after a few weeks of training them, I felt completely free to sleep in another room five nights a week. Paul and I each had one night watch per week. The person on night watch would spend the night on the couch in the living room, and got up every two hours to see how Anne was doing, and usually suctioned her as well. Anne became well accustomed to this rhythm, and almost never woke up during suctioning.

September went by quickly. Paul and I did not have to contact another intensive care unit. We watched the length of the catheter very carefully, as well as its position. The diagonal cut of the lower end of the tube needed to be oriented toward the left main stem bronchus. We could not afford the slightest error in either length or rotation.

After several weeks, as we became accustomed to the system, we were not as vigilant. In order to remain attentive, we created data sheets divided into hours, similar to those at the hospital. We noted humidity levels, suctioning frequency, food intake, times of vomiting, cardiac frequency and position of the catheter.

All of this required good organization, considerable time, and much attention to detail. I had only one patient but, contrary to being in the hospital, I did everything, from housecleaning to tube care. I was the only day team, assisted by Paul, seven days a week.

I ran my errands when Paul was home to watch Anne, which was less frequent during working hours now that he had his office at the Bible Institute. [1]

Anne had no medication to take, but we used three bottles of normal saline per day, for the irrigation of catheters, as well as two bottles of distilled water for the humidifier. This amounted to 150 half-quart bottles to buy from the pharmacy each month!

---

[1] Paul was now working as Academic Dean at the Nogent Bible Institute near Paris.

We also had to reorganize the respiratory therapy appointments. We were happy to find Joel, a competent and friendly local respiratory therapist, who became our friend. He came every day, including Sundays. When Anne was congested, he came twice a day.

The respiratory therapy sessions were uncomfortable and tiring for Anne. She regularly fell asleep on the table while the therapist was exerting very strong manual pressure on her chest. Seeing her fall asleep in this fashion was surprising and somewhat frightening! She seemed to have lost consciousness, but she had simply fallen asleep. I think she found refuge from this exhausting experience by being absent. She usually woke up soon after the end of the session.

Despite my fatigue and the tension linked to Anne's situation, I felt much better now that she was at home. I had brightened up and put on some weight.

Several colleagues agreed to relieve me of most of my medical work in the schools that year. I was allowed to work only half a day, every other week. This was not enough to keep us eligible for national health insurance benefits. But under the circumstances, and after numerous letters, telephone calls and medical certificates, all Anne's medical expenses continued to be covered, including Home Care services. [2]

On September 10, I gave my daughter her first immunizations, which had purposefully not been given until then. Though she protested of course, it gave me satisfaction to immunize her. For once, this was a medical intervention unrelated to her specific condition. It put her in the same category as normal children. It was also a gesture that represented confidence in the future!

October came and the ICU reopened, completely renovated. We had held on! Even better, we were now convinced we were capable of keeping Anne home permanently. The attempt had been successful! Some doctors and nurses told us privately they thought a lot

---

[2]   We calculated that Anne's first year of health care cost the national health system the equivalent of over one million U.S. dollars!

about Anne during their vacation and worried about her. Now they were the ones worrying about not seeing her!

A great chapter in our life ended. Anne was not healed, but we had gone through the eye of the hurricane, and had come out of it not much the worse for wear.

During this first year in Anne's life, my activities were significantly reduced. I was unable to make plans, even a day ahead of time. I was caught within the four walls of a hospital bedroom.

Paradoxically, it was the most fruitful year of my life. I received an accelerated learning experience from the Lord. He set me apart and had molded me into a different person, a more useful instrument in His hands.

The Apostle Peter, speaking to suffering Christians, explained the process of growth through trials:

"And the God of all grace, who called you to his eternal glory in Christ, after you have suffered a little while, will himself restore you and make you strong, firm and steadfast." [3]

Happiness and Freedom

It is well-known that the greatest joys follow the deepest sorrows. In the Fall of 1982, our family was the happiest in the world. Our happiness could be summed up in a few words; we were together, all four of us, at home! We no longer took life nor simply living together as a family for granted. Our little Anne had just been given back to us for her first birthday, after spending a year in intensive care.

The Lord guided us step by step through these stormy months. We now felt ready, knowing He was at our side, for the great adventure of living together, as well as possible considering Anne's handicap.

---

[3] I Peter 5:10.

Anne had been home since August 25th. With much patience, we had succeeded in feeding her with the bottle. In October, I finally managed to get her to swallow half a cup of applesauce. She took about thirty minutes to eat this tiny meal. I had learned in the past few months not to measure my actions in terms of speed or effectiveness. Half an hour after this success, she threw up. I had to teach her the swallowing reflex as patiently as I could.

I never asked myself if I was doing the right thing. I never asked if it might be a better idea for me to practice medicine, rather than to exhaust myself helping only Anne, my daughter, who perhaps might not live. Moreover, we could have placed Anne in an institution. But I knew I was where God wanted me when taking care of her and I was happy to be with her. God was victorious! Our friends from the Saint-Gilles ICU, as well as our Christian friends, had supported us throughout the ordeal. Anne was really, in a way, a child who belonged to all of us.

A new chapter of our lives was beginning. Without knowing where we were headed, we remained confident.

A Near Catastrophe

At the end of November, Anne suffered severe bronchitis, and began to bleed through her tube. The irritated and swollen airway prevented the air from moving freely, and she began wheezing. The frequent suctioning brought up dirty, bloody and sometimes purulent secretions, which threatened to obstruct her airway at any time. From a medical point of view, I felt completely alone. I was Anne's mother and the treating physician at the same time. Who could I call for help?

Only the Intensive Care team would be able to help me. I frequently called them by telephone. They were always patient and attentive. Yet I knew that the role of the intensivists at large Parisian hospitals was not to follow up on their former patients, especially by telephone. I sometimes thought about consulting a local pediatrician.

But what good would that do? He or she would not be acquainted with Anne's problem, would never have known a similar case, and would not treat her any better than I would.

One day in December we came extremely close to a catastrophe. I was sitting by the fireplace, holding Anne on my lap. I was reading her a story. Suddenly I noticed that Anne was not breathing. I did not feel her breath on my hand placed in front of her tube. Her face was marked by surprise and pain. I immediately ran to her room, laid her down on the changing table, and forcefully instilled several syringes of normal saline in her trach tube, but no mucous plugs came out. She was already becoming ashen. Paul rushed to help me when he heard my cries. He suggested, for the lack of another solution, we change the trach tube. When faced with an emergency, my hands did not operate as easily as they did when I had rehearsed this at the hospital. My mind was paralyzed by fear. My hands were trembling. Paul remained calm. In my haze I heard him say, "Here are the scissors, here's a number four catheter."

I was usually the leader when it came to Anne's health, but that day I obeyed his orders and acted like a robot. Anne was a few seconds away from death. I gave my confused mind and trembling hands to the Lord, "Lord, do it for me because I don't know what to do!"

The string broke as I awkwardly cut with the scissors. I yanked the tube out. The lower part of the tube was plugged by a blood clot and some mucous. I was reassured. We knew exactly the cause of the respiratory arrest. Anne began to breathe weakly. I quickly inserted a new trach tube. When I tried to give her oxygen, I could not connect the hose nor use the facemask. Finally, I manually directed the flow of oxygen toward her new tube. I realized I would have to be much better prepared the next time!

Anne regained her color. She fell asleep in my arms. When she awakened, I tested her psychomotor abilities. She had lost none of her capacities. We thanked God once again for sparing Anne's life and brain.

We learned several useful lessons. We now avoided lighting a fire in our fireplace when Anne was congested. As warm and cozy as a fire was during this season, it dried the air, which was very dangerous for Anne. We purchased several humidifiers as well as a hygrometer.

After this incident, I realized the extent we had to rely on our own resources. I had the telephone number of an ICU ambulance posted in Anne's room, but these things happen so quickly that it is an illusion to count on external help in case of emergency.

America – So Far Away!

On December 15, Anne went back to the hospital for a bronchoscopy. Six months had gone by since the previous one. We hoped the condition of her trachea had improved. Unfortunately, Dr. Tristan told us there was no change in the damaged area. We made an appointment for another bronchoscopy in June. It was useless to try anything until then.

It seemed so easy for Dr. Tristan to set an appointment in six months! For Anne, it meant six more months of precarious health, waiting for improvement.

We enjoyed our holidays nonetheless. It was Anne's first Christmas at home as well as the anniversary of her critical operation. Anne's 81-year old great-grandmother, Amé, came to spend a few weeks with us. It was a joy to see my grandmother take pleasure in reading the Bible and praying. At 81, she began to understand the difference between being religious and knowing God personally. She became calmer, more patient, more attentive to others. The Spirit of God was at work in her heart.

Paul left for a three-week trip to the United States. January was difficult for me. I had to overcome ideas of self-pity, and even injustice and revolt. I was jealous because Paul continued to work, to travel, and to lead a relatively normal life. I felt I was doing nothing either useful or enjoyable. At the same time, I knew that my constant care for Anne was an investment in her future, even though her future remained quite uncertain.

My trust in the Lord and my deep conviction that I was doing the right thing were of great help to me. I knew that even if I found someone to stay with Anne so that I could go to work, I would not be happy. It was preferable to bear up under this difficult situation, finding in God the resources that I needed day by day.

Paul's return was a great joy. I expressed my discouragement and frustrations to him. I was again able to leave the house whenever he was there to watch over Anne. Together we witnessed our daughter's first steps at the age of 17 months. After such a long hospitalization, she was making up for lost time.

A Nearly Fatal Mistake

After the first sunny days of February, we took Anne outside, wearing a heavy winter coat and a hood. She developed several infectious episodes which were very difficult for all of us. The pale winter sun was not yet warm enough for her outings.

In the mornings, Anne was always congested when she woke up, but I did not suction her immediately. I preferred giving her a bottle, and then a long humidifying bath, so that the secretions that had accumulated during the night could detach themselves from the tube. This way, Anne learned to unplug her own airway by coughing. I would then clean the tube by performing my own respiratory therapy as well as a long session of suctioning.

I usually performed these morning tasks myself. I only left Anne with Paul or Sylvie, the nurse on call, when Anne was breathing well.

One Wednesday morning, however, I made a mistake that was nearly fatal. At 9:00 am, I accompanied Matthieu to his judo class, then returned home right away. I was absent only about 10 minutes and Paul was home. As soon as I came in, I was alerted by his urgent voice, "Anne is not well, we are in her room."

I rushed to her room and found Paul strongly compressing Anne's chest in an attempt to expel an obstruction. Anne was not breathing at all. I approached and saw her lose consciousness completely. Her eyes rolled back. Her body arched and became rigid. I envisioned her already dead, and I was struck by a violent fear; in a few seconds, it would be all over. These 18 months were going to end!

In my distress, I called out audibly, "Lord, do something!" Could I believe in a miracle, at this time? I looked frantically for the scissors. They were not there... still a few more seconds... Paul came back from the kitchen with another pair of scissors and I was finally able to pull out the plugged tube. She immediately stopped convulsing, but I could not feel her breath, and she was not regaining consciousness.

I tried inserting a new tube; it did not seem to improve the situation. Was there still a plug in the trachea? What more could I do? I felt powerless in the face of death, which was settling in second by second. I visualized a precious vase falling down, and my powerlessness to catch it. Could it be that all there was left to do was to give up and cry? I vaguely heard Paul's voice: "Try to slide the tube up and down in the trachea to break the plug."

I pushed the trach tube a little bit further, and moved it back and forth in the trachea, like a corkscrew. At the same time, Paul was instilling in the tube enough water to drown her! Anne, unconscious, was unable to cough.

I stopped my movement for an instant to use the suction machine and put it on maximum power! I could not worry about damaging the tracheal walls. We had no choice. Suddenly long, stringy filaments of secretions appeared at the end of the suction catheter, obstructing it completely.

Anne began to breathe and regained consciousness. Everything had lasted less than three minutes. I immediately directed the oxygen toward her tube. I spoke to Anne, to make sure she could respond. She understood. Her brain seemed undamaged. Completely exhausted, she fell asleep. Paul and I sat at the end of the bed. We thanked God for the miracle of Anne's life, for the fact that I had not stayed to chat with other moms at the gym where I had dropped Matthieu off, that I had not had to stop for a red light on the way home, and that we were both present at the critical moment. Wednesday was the only weekday that Paul stayed home in the morning!

A few minutes later, Anne was sleeping well with her new tube. I went to pick up Matthieu, surprised our life was continuing as if nothing had happened. I chatted a few minutes with other moms, then helped Matthieu tie his shoes, vaguely listening to his carefree chatter. I thought to myself, "What would this moment be like, if things hadn't worked out? How would I have spoken to Matthieu? How would I have told my parents? Why can dropping one's guard for a moment threaten an entire life, destroying 18 months of effort?"

Then a Bible verse came to my mind, and it helped me to dispel these dark thoughts:

> *"Finally, brothers, whatever is true, whatever is noble, whatever is right, whatever is pure, whatever is lovely, whatever is admirable – if anything is excellent or praiseworthy – think about such things... And the God of peace will be with you."* [4]

The dark thoughts I had were neither true (since none of it had happened) nor lovely. Therefore, they did not please God, and could not come from Him. Instead, I had to focus my attention on useful and positive things: thanking God for His protection, drawing useful lessons from this crisis. I really needed to appropriate the promise that concluded this verse: "... and the God of peace will be with you."

---

[4] Philippians 4:8-9.

Chapter 11
Learning a New Life

S pring came along, bringing ideal weather for an extubation attempt. On May 4, 1983, Anne was admitted to Saint-Gilles hospital for a bronchoscopy. Six months had passed since the previous one and we thought that Anne might now be able to live without her tracheal tube. Yet we had become so accustomed to failure that we did not dare hope. The ICU team seemed to believe in success more than we did. Indeed, it had been nearly a year since Anne had left the unit.

The bronchoscopy took place in the ENT unit in Saint-Gilles hospital, the oldest and most rundown part of the hospital. I waited for the results of this examination, praying for Anne's safety. I still dreaded the dangers of general anesthesia and of potential damage caused by the bronchoscope. These immediate fears momentarily eclipsed hopes for Anne's long-term improvement.

After a seemingly endless time, Dr. Tristan came out of the operating room. His calmness reassured me immediately. The procedure went well but the news was not very good. The condition of the trachea had not really changed. Nevertheless, he recommended bringing the tube up progressively, five millimeters at a time, to see if Anne could do without it. I could do this at home, allowing me to choose the most opportune time.

The bronchoscopy caused a severe inflammatory reaction. Anne coughed and began to bleed through her tube. I had to put her on antibiotics and wait for better days to begin experimenting. I was in no hurry, and was happy to schedule these attempts myself, according to Anne's clinical condition.

It was on June 3 that I judged her condition sufficiently stable and satisfactory to try pulling up the tube. I made this attempt at night, hoping to profit from the time Anne would be asleep, so I could observe her more easily. At the age of two, she now ran everywhere and it was difficult to keep her calm and quiet during the day.

I pulled the tube up nine millimeters at 8:30 pm. Anne went to sleep quietly. At midnight, her breathing became wheezy. I pushed

Anne at age two.

the tube back down four millimeters. The rest of the night went very well. We had gained five millimeters. At 1:00 pm the next day, I brought the tube up two more millimeters. At 7:30 pm, she had a bad mucous plug, and I had to slide it back down. I left it in its low position for the night in order to sleep, and began my attempts again the next day.

Anne seemed to tolerate these experiments rather well at first, but she became more congested after a while, and could not expel the secretions. A few days later, we put an end to the experiments and drew a few conclusions from them. The trachea would remain sufficiently wide during the first hours, then would begin to gradually close, keeping the secretions from coming out, thus creating a plug. The plug formed an obstacle to the airway. We agreed with the intensive care team not to attempt a complete extubation. Everyone believed complete extubation would be doomed to failure. And so the long road of patience and prayer continued.

One positive thing remained; Anne was now capable of living for several hours with her tube in a higher position, which meant that an error in the positioning of the tube would not be as life-threatening as it had been before. Still, the daily risk of infection and clogging remained.

Summer 1983 came and we decided to leave for a vacation, despite all the complications this would mean. It was necessary for us to resist discouragement and our reaction was to try to live as if Anne were not handicapped. We did not deny her handicap, but wanted to adapt to it to the best we could.

Toward the end of August, we left for two weeks at the Ile of Groix, a small island off the coast of Brittany. Was it foolish on our part to leave for such an isolated location with no hospitals close by? After thinking about this question for a while, we realized that it mattered little where we spent our vacation, since we were independent, and no hospital except for Saint-Gilles would really be able to help us anyway. I nevertheless asked Anne's doctors for their opinion, and they confirmed what I believed: We were the only ones who were specifically equipped to take care of Anne, and we were the only ones familiar with her situation. We were free to go wherever we wished, so why not a tiny isolated island off the Brittany coast?

During our vacation, while Anne still refused to be spoon-fed any form of solid food, we saw her pick up peas that had fallen on the ground and put them in her mouth. We then tried to give her some on a plate and encouraged her to eat, but she resolutely refused to touch them! Our next idea was to leave a few peas on the coffee table. She enjoyed picking them up and eating them. On August 25, her second birthday, she agreed to be spoon-fed mashed potatoes and ground meat.

Her respiratory condition was now becoming more stable, so we stopped maintaining hourly records as we had done previously. Anne was now two years old. We had become independent, weaned from the hospital. Because we had gone through so many critical moments during the year, we now felt more capable of facing emergency situations. We used the humidifier only during the night, we could now give Anne respiratory therapy ourselves, and she had begun to talk!

Looking back at Anne's past year, we were happy to see the immense progress that had been made, though we would have liked even more. We previously believed that success depended solely on being freed from the tube. Yet now we could see that Anne lived better with it, making it easier to wait for the time when extubation would finally be possible. And was it not more important to live fully in the present, rather than in constant apprehension of the future? Healthy people tend to believe that the happiness of handicapped individuals is dependent on being freed from their handicap. Yet we were learning that the quality of life mattered more than anything! This helped us to see the future in very different terms. The Lord would guide us step by step. If Anne was to be extubated, it would happen at the right time, according to God's will. This might not be very soon. If surgery was necessary, God would guide us as well. If she was to keep her tracheotomy her entire life, a frightening prospect right then, God could still give us all strength for living life fully. Our greatest joy was to see how well Anne was coping with her situation. She was joyful, full of life, and patient when it came to the tiring respiratory therapy and suctioning sessions (which were made a little easier thanks to Daddy's funny stories and faces). She smiled easily and endeared herself to all.

Ironically, the situation was more difficult for Matthieu than it was for Anne. He continued to be a melancholy dreamer. He began to toy with Anne's used suction catheters, while telling imaginary stories to himself. He spent entire hours doing this and did not have any interest whatsoever in construction games or toy cars, unlike most four-year old boys. His relationship with Anne was alternately gentle or aggressive. He ignored her most of the time, lost in the stories he was making up.

It was difficult for him to express his feelings, although one day he did suggest throwing Anne out the car window onto the highway. We understood his logical reaction and, though we were happy that he had felt free to express his opinion, we calmly explained that little sisters could not be thrown out of cars, even when they required so much attention! His remark made us realize even more clearly how difficult the situation was for him. He had probably been suppressing feelings of hostility towards his sister, mixed with fear that she might not do well, which would cause Mommy and Daddy a lot of pain.

Was it this anxiety that led him to flee to his imaginary world? Was his playing with the catheters of any significance?

We understood we had to be especially attentive to Matthieu's needs. We needed to encourage him and help him feel good about himself. It became obvious that he wished to become sick so that he too might attract our attention. We therefore had to give him attention before he invented an imaginary disease. We did not, however, completely succeed.

A Gamble

The beginning of the new school year established the rhythm for our schedules. I went back to work four mornings a week. Our friend Sylvie, a nurse, stayed with Anne. I was able to regain an active life and normalize my relationship with Anne, which until then had been too exclusive, too intense.

I rented a pager so Sylvie could contact me anywhere and at any time. All of the schools where I worked were within a ten-minute drive from our house. Still, I feared the prospect of working regular hours.

Paul suggested that I return to my medical studies, to prepare for a medical specialty. It was a major gamble to combine part-time work with difficult studies and two children, one of whom was handicapped. This plan tempted me nevertheless. I knew I would not be satisfied very long, professionally speaking, with medical visits to junior high schools. I decided to specialize in industrial medicine. It was certainly not the most prestigious specialty, but could be practiced part-time, which is more compatible with family life. The classes were in Paris, two afternoons a week. I could be reached by pager, but it would take more than an hour for me to get home. The major risk for Anne was still the formation of a plug, so I showed Sylvie how to change the catheter in case of emergency.

I had mixed feelings about my new plans. Was it selfish of me to leave my children two evenings a week? Was I taking a major risk

for very personal motives? Or rather, was it not time for me to realize that I was not indispensable at home?

My classes began in October. I always carried my pager and
called home between classes. I succeeded in concentrating on my
studies without being constantly preoccupied with Anne's situation.

Grueling Winter Nights

A new bronchoscopy performed at the end of October revealed no
progress. What could we do except wait, always wait? We gathered
our strength to face a third winter with the trach tube. My friend
Maria came from Morocco for a few days and encouraged us as best
she could. The bonds formed in the ICU were still very much alive.
Like war veterans, we reminisced over the winter of 1982 when we
had been together in the ICU.

The winter was more trying than the summer. Anne, now 14
months, had numerous infectious episodes that were still worrisome.
When she was not doing well, I stayed in her room the whole night.
When her coughing produced heavy secretions, I suctioned her
sometimes every single minute for an hour. Sometimes, the highly
inflamed tissues bled and she bled considerably through her tube. I
would then instill a few drops of steroid solution directly into her trachea in an attempt to stop this dangerous bleeding. Blood, when dry,
could impede the passing of air through the trachea. I had learned
this technique in the ICU. The instillation had to be made one drop
at a time and during Anne's sleep, otherwise she would immediately cough everything out. I would instill a drop, wait half an hour,
then instill a second drop, hoping she would keep it down.
Sometimes, she not only coughed out the medicine, but also vomited her entire dinner.

When the bleeding stopped, I would lie down on a mat next to her,
her hand in mine, and sing lullabies until she went to sleep. When
she was asleep, I took my Bible, and read the promises of God's protection. In the same way my daughter felt protected in my presence,

I felt safe in the presence of my heavenly Father. I would fall asleep then, only to be awakened by Anne's first cough. These coughing episodes were sometimes only a few minutes apart. The unproductive fits of coughing were the most nerve-wracking. Nothing could make them stop. Tracheal suctioning was useless and actually worsened the situation.

Anne sometimes coughed like this for several hours. I tried to reposition the humidifier, closer, further, or to get her to drink, but nothing worked. These fits usually ceased in the early morning. Anne and I then slept for a few hours. Next I had to prepare Matthieu for school and, finally, go to work myself as soon as Sylvie arrived. We had now hired Sylvie privately for daytime care. I maintained contact with Sylvie the whole morning by telephone. Fortunately, not all nights were so demanding. By now, Home Care had reduced their service to only two nights a week. Whenever an infectious episode persisted, Paul came to take over in the middle of the night.

Moments of Depression

At the end of winter, I went through a terrible time of depression. Anne was doing rather well. I suddenly released all the nervous tension that I had accumulated over the previous two years. During those days, I had been anxious and nervous, but not depressed. At present, I experienced less anxiety concerning Anne, because the threat of her death had significantly decreased.

This depression manifested itself through insomnia the nights I did not have to take care of Anne. Then, I began to suffer from relentless headaches. My imagination turned these symptoms into a morbid story in which I would assuredly die of a serious disease. Anne would do well, but I would die. This became an obsession. Recognizing that such fears had no logical basis, I tried to combat them with all my might.

I had forgotten that it is impossible to fight against the powers of evil alone. I felt powerless and guilty. I was a victim of the great

accuser, the enemy of God. I could no longer concentrate on anything. The idea of my imminent death invaded me completely and
left no room for anything else. I became inefficient in my responsibilities as wife, mother and medical student. Was I projecting on
myself the fear of death I had felt for Anne for two years? Every single day, I tried as hard as I could to convince myself that my troubles were solely psychological. I felt as though I was no longer a
single cohesive person. On one level, I considered the problem rationally, yet on another level, I was unable to convince myself. I waited quite some time before seeking help. I felt weak and ridiculous,
and did not want to be considered a "psycho case," to use medical
slang.

Life became so difficult that I could not concentrate on my family anymore. This added a feeling of guilt to my anxiety. I felt I was
a bad wife and a bad mother. My insomnia led me to a state of constant fatigue, which supported my idea that I was very seriously ill.
I was in the middle of a vicious circle of depression.

Of course, I prayed to the Lord to help me, but because I tried to
rescue myself from the crisis rather than admit my powerlessness to
do so, I became more and more hopelessly tangled into my depression, and thus kept the Holy Spirit from working in me.

I came to the end of my rope, finally recognizing my weakness
and allowing myself to be humbled before God and man. When I lost
my inhibition to appear depressed, when I was no longer ashamed to
cry with my close friends, when I removed my mask of invincibility
and allowed the real me to appear, the situation began to untangle.

I resolved to consult a fellow doctor about my headaches. The
very fact that I went through X-rays and laboratory examination had
a beneficial effect. I was admitting I had symptoms, instead of
repressing them.

I spoke to Paul at length. I had not done so before because I was
afraid to bore and confuse him with my physical and psychological
problems. His gracious listening helped me as well. He felt rather

powerless to help me, but the very fact that he listened without judging did me a lot of good.

Paul advised me to meet with a pastor friend of ours who often served as a counselor in our church. I set my pride aside and went to this friend in my weakness, even though I had always wanted to appear to him as a strong woman who was able to withstand adversity. How difficult it was!

Our friend graciously accepted to help me and I saw him twice a week for a few weeks. He had me write a list every morning of all the things that I wanted to thank God for, and another list of the things that were not going well. Every day hence I wrote down my anxieties, my fears of the future, my headaches and my insomnia. Likewise, I always did my best to write down the positive elements of the situation. I would note if Anne had spent a good night or if the weather was nice. I thanked God for this positive list and entrusted the negative one to Him, asking Him to carry my burdens.

At first, I had to force myself to find reasons to be thankful. But little by little, the list of good things became longer. I was able to thank God for a better night, for half a day without headaches, for the help I had obtained from my counselor, for the support of my husband, and for the promises of peace found in the Bible. The negative thoughts that pervaded my soul were replaced by more positive ones. The vicious circle of depression began to break. I was far from being completely healed, but the worst was over. Being less anxious and worried, I began to sleep better. The headaches continued for quite a while. The examinations had revealed nothing, therefore I resolved not to inquire any further into any of the medical aspects.

In order to combat the invasion of my soul by negative thoughts, I memorized Bible passages. One verse especially seemed to contain the answer to my problem and began with the following words:

> *"Finally, be strong in the Lord and his mighty power."* [1]

---

[1] Ephesians 6:10-18.

I was without strength, and needed to find it in a source other than myself. The Lord has strength without limits from which I could freely draw if I were in union with him. How could I find this union? I could find it through prayer, through meditation upon His Word, and by speaking and listening to Him when I was in great need, certainly several times a day during that period.

I felt the need to be free from all responsibilities for a time. The stress that built up as I watched over Anne, the burdens of my regular role as wife and mother, as well as the intellectual effort I needed for my studies, had all pushed me beyond my limits.

In late March, I had a wonderful opportunity to go to a ski camp in the French Alps. I could go there with Matthieu and my aunt Monique. I had to come to the very end of my psychological resources to leave Anne. Sylvie would come every day to help Paul.

I left, wondering once again whether I was selfish and careless to leave my main responsibility; Anne's survival. The time in the mountains was wonderful. I added many things to my daily list of positive events!

I left tired and still burdened by my headaches, but I was on the right track. The director of this camp for adults had asked me to be the doctor of the camp, but I had to refuse, risking being misunderstood. I did not have the strength to be responsible for anything. Even when skiing, I let others choose the trails. I avoided any decision-making. The director and my friends there were very understanding. The Bible studies were interesting and lively, and I had the joy of seeing my aunt discover a personal relationship with God. Once again, in acknowledging my weakness. I came home healed, freed from headaches and anxiety for the first time in three months.

As soon as I returned home, I had to begin working intensely on my final exams. I finally felt able to concentrate on my studies. It brought back memories of my carefree student years and I began to realize how this long trial had influenced my views on life. I knew I would never ever be the same. Compared to my student years, I saw studying in a different light. Before, there were exams to pass and challenges to meet. Now studying was a privilege, a joy, even a means of relaxation.

The days preceding the qualifying exam for Industrial Medicine were mentally strenuous, but also very stimulating. I longed for a return to "normal" life, spending more time with my children, and the daily routine as a housewife. We are such complicated beings, so difficult to satisfy! I was trying to find that delicate balance between the stimulation of my mind and the satisfaction of being home with my family.

Third Birthday

On June 15, 1984, we attempted to remove Anne's tube, but once again this failed. It was very difficult to keep believing there was a possibility of success. Every year, for the last three years, each experience resembled the previous one; a few hours of hope and then rapid deterioration. Every time we experienced the dilemma of either letting her suffer longer or allowing her to rest. Allowing her to rest meant giving up the hope and knowledge we gained from prolonging the procedure. Of course, we always ended up reinserting the tube.

On August 25, we celebrated Anne's third birthday with a family outing to a park in Boulogne, near Paris. It was wonderful to see Anne climbing ropes, driving little electric boats, and jumping in sandboxes! When Anne was in the hospital, we had never imagined that she could live so normally with a tracheotomy!

Anne at the beach, age three.

In September, we left for a vacation in southern France. It seemed like we had to take an entire mobile clinic with us, because of all the medical equipment we needed, but what a reward! Some friends loaned us a comfortable house on the bank of a small river. We went on long hikes, carrying Anne in a rucksack most of the way. Here at least, her slow weight gain was advantageous!

Chapter 12

A Story of Perseverance

"Let us not become weary in doing good, for at the proper time we will reap a harvest if we do not give up." [1]

In the fall of 1984, a Christian women's group asked me to speak about my experiences with Anne's illness. For the first time, I felt free to talk about it in public without feeling that I was betraying a secret between God and me. I was now happy to share the joy of God's faithfulness over the past months and years. One of our great joys was to hear Anne speak increasingly better. Her tracheal tube still measured only about 3.5 millimeters (1/8 inch) in diameter. The increased size of her windpipe left enough room for some air to circulate around the tube as well as in it. Some months previous, when Anne was two, we realized that she oddly lowered her head when she spoke. As we observed her more closely, we saw she covered the opening of her tube with her chin. This technique kept the air from passing through the tube, forcing it to pass around it and through the vocal cords. Anne would lift her head to catch her breath, then lower it again to cover the tube and resume her conversation, three-year-old-style! Her personally developed technique impressed Dr. Tristan, her ENT specialist.

Another Winter

The Paris winter of 1984-85 was harsh. Snow fell heavily and we built a large snowman on our terrace. Three-year old Anne could enjoy the snowman from the window.

---

[1] Galatians 6:9.

In February, Anne underwent a seventh bronchoscopy. Again the fibrous condition of the tracheal walls was unchanged. X-rays showed significant over-inflation of the left lung. I worried this might eventually be dangerous for her only lung. Was her lung deteriorating little by little? Was Anne slowly dying? Instead of healing was she developing chronic respiratory insufficiency? No one really knew. A computerized angiogram was performed. This procedure showed normal blood flow within her one lung. This reassured us somewhat.

The inner diameter of the trachea was about 3 millimeters at its narrowest segment. The doctors attempted to stretch this narrowed area by inserting a larger tube and pushing it down very low, all the way to the opening of the main bronchus. An attempt to remove it would then be made in June.

During this long winter we established a custom we never regretted: "family evenings." Once a week, we devoted our time to activities with our children. Paul made this a priority and accepted no appointments or meetings for those times. Even so, our "family evenings" were often disturbed by a telephone call. We began to unplug the phone for a few hours in order to fully devote ourselves to our children in this special time. We played games, did crafts, or had musical evenings. Anne liked to hide in the guitar case, into which she fit completely!

Matthieu's Suffering

Easter weekend brought quite an unpleasant surprise. On Wednesday morning, Matthieu, now five, woke up with a locked knee. He could barely walk. I tried to determine if he had hurt himself the day before, but he had not. I examined his knee. There was no visible sign of damage of any kind. I kept him home, hoping his knee would gradually get better. I suspected he was capitalizing on a little bump he had in order to get our attention. Paul and I had noticed that he was having an increasingly hard time in his last year of pre-school, despite his precocious ability to read. Was he looking for a way to escape from school?

He stayed home, lying on the floor of his room, keeping busy by reading books. There was no improvement the next day. I watched him from the corner of my eye, thinking he would end up betraying his pretense. Instead, even when he thought that he was alone, he stood up with difficulty and his knee remained locked in flexion. He did not complain about any pain, but simply said he could not move his leg.

This was beginning to exasperate me. I had to force myself to be patient enough to help him move around. Matthieu was suffering, either in his body or in his psyche, and I did not know how to help him. I became more and more impatient, which did not help the situation at all.

On the third day, Good Friday, he declared that he could not get up at all. His other knee was locked as well! I was worried and exasperated as well, but I tried not to show it. I gently tried to help him stretch his legs, but to no avail. The limbs were blocked at about sixty degrees of flexion. It was out of the question for him to even limp, he now had to be carried, even to go to the bathroom. He had become entirely dependent on us, even for the most elementary things. Was this what he unconsciously longed for?

There was still no sign of any physical trauma or pain. We tried to reassure our Matthieu, to tell him that his legs would soon work again. We prayed with him. Nothing changed! On Saturday, I went to the hospital to consult an orthopedic surgeon. We could no longer ignore the problem. Matthieu was brought to the examination room in a wheelchair, and was carried by an orderly to the examination table. I was perplexed and asked myself why I now had a second child in the hospital! The possibility of a serious disease vaguely came to mind, but I dismissed it immediately. We would live this new adventure one day at a time as well!

The orthopedic surgeon briefly examined Matthieu, observing the same strong, rigid contractions that kept his legs from stretching nor-

mally. After a few seconds, he told me that this was almost certainly a case of "pathomimic." This meant that there was no actual physical injury, but that this was an imitation of a disease. In other words,
this was all going on in the mind of my six-year old son. Was this
good or bad news? Before, I always had a tendency to take mental
illnesses less seriously than physical diseases, but after my own
struggle with depression, I was no longer certain they were any less
serious.

Matthieu was laid down on a bed. His legs were attached to
weights that applied traction through cables and pulleys. We hoped
this would gradually reduce the contraction of his legs. The surgeon
decided that this procedure should last four hours. He would then
decide whether Matthieu could return home. I felt sorry for my little
boy. I had a difficult time admitting that all this paraphernalia was
necessary for an illness that did not really exist. Outside of
Matthieu's presence, I asked the doctor about the significance of
such symptoms. He told me it was not rare for children to manifest
mental anguish by physical symptoms, but that this most often took
the form of stomach cramps rather than locked limbs. He was optimistic. He told us it was necessary to treat Matthieu's symptoms, to
reassure him and to avoid telling him there was nothing wrong. After
the traction, he should undergo physical therapy to help him relax his
muscles and to reassure him by showing him that he was being taken
care of.

When I explained Anne's disease to the surgeon, he immediately
put two and two together; Matthieu was mimicking a pathological
condition, because he subconsciously reproached Anne for having
been ill so long, requiring so much of our attention.

Matthieu spent Easter Sunday of 1985 in traction in a hospital
bed. It was very distressing for me to leave him alone there. We had
been invited to the home of some friends and we found ourselves in
the odd situation of taking Anne to our friends' home and leaving
Matthieu at the hospital!

We talked a long time about what we should do for Matthieu. We
would spend more time with him alone. We would talk less about

Anne's condition in his presence. This was difficult, because her situation was such an essential part of our lives. We did not want it to become taboo. We would at least have to talk about it without fear, and as naturally as possible.

The next day, when we arrived at the hospital, one of the two knees functioned normally. This was the first progress in a week! Matthieu began limping around the room again. The other limb had improved somewhat, and the physician decided to discharge our son with an anti-anxiety treatment for a month, combined with daily sessions of physical therapy. The physical therapist who came to help Anne release her secretions also took care of Matthieu's knees. Our son was finally on par with his sister.

The Story of Mimi

We had promised Matthieu a small pet to celebrate his discharge from the hospital. Now the time had come to keep our promise. We decided together we would buy a guinea pig, thinking this would not mean too much work. But how were we to find a guinea pig on Easter Sunday? All of the pet shops near the suburban hospital were closed. We had to go to Paris to find a shopkeeper on the banks of the Seine, where Matthieu found a young female guinea pig, which he immediately adopted and named "Mimi."

Mimi's story was brief and sad, but left us with an unforgettable memory. Mimi had time to participate in only one of our "family evenings." A week after her arrival at our house, I found her lying on her side, gasping. I know nothing about animals, but this seemed to be rather bad news. Was this a case of acute respiratory distress in a guinea pig?

What could we do? This little animal was supposed to improve things in our home, not complicate them further! I now had a daughter with a tracheotomy, a limping son, and a dying guinea pig! I knew Matthieu was deeply anguished by the fear of sickness and death. We had adopted an animal to reassure him, following the advice of several well-intentioned friends. But Mimi seemed to be betraying us, ready to die before our eyes.

The children saw that Mimi was ill. Matthieu became very worried. I had to take the guinea pig out of his sight, or he would have suffered intensely from his powerlessness in the face of death. When I told the children I was taking Mimi to the veterinarian, Matthieu was immediately relieved. I mainly wanted Matthieu to avoid seeing Mimi's imminent demise. I had never gone to a veterinarian, and I wondered if they even treated guinea pigs.

The situation suddenly appeared both humorous and absurd. The vet's waiting room was full. I sat on the only unoccupied chair, with my small cardboard box on my lap. I peeked inside. Mimi was still breathing, but seemed in very bad shape. By that time, I felt quite certain that veterinarians did not treat guinea pigs. All the other animals in the waiting room were dogs and cats which, as a matter of fact, did not look sick at all. Was I to wait or announce the emergency?

I waited a long time feeling more and more exasperated. Every once in a while I looked in the box to see whether the guinea pig was still alive. I was tempted to give up and leave, but I thought of Matthieu, at home, who was anxiously waiting for news. Several customers went in before me. One last look at Mimi; she was neither moving nor breathing.

I was about to leave when the door opened. It was my turn! What could I do? Should I pay a veterinarian to tell me I had a dead guinea pig in my cardboard box? The situation was turning tragically comic. I entered the consulting room and said half-jokingly: "Uh, I think it's a little late!" I opened the box and displayed the dead guinea pig. If she was laughing on the inside, the veterinarian certainly did not show it. She told me our guinea pig probably died of acute gastroenteritis. We both gravely considered the hopeless situation. Just so that she could do something, I suppose, she performed a rapid autopsy which confirmed the diagnosis.

"Did you feed it wet salad?" she asked me. "That can cause fatal cases of gastroenteritis in rodents." I did not know what to answer. We had given Mimi salad from the refrigerator, but had it been wet?

The young woman proposed to get rid of the corpse for me and did not charge me for the consultation. I was very relieved not to have to bring the dead animal back to the children, which would spare me a funeral in the back yard. I drove back home, mentally rehearsing the best way to tell them the bad news. I really did not have much choice; as soon as I returned, I calmly told them that Mimi had died at the veterinarian's, and that the vet had kept her.

Matthieu cried bitterly. Anne was not really affected by the news. I consoled Matthieu as well as I could, and promised him another pet, more hardy this time. A few days later, Matthieu chose a black and white kitten. I hoped it would last longer than the guinea pig.

Our Mobile Home Clinic

Anne underwent another bronchoscopy on June 6. We hoped the new tube, with its larger diameter, would have helped the trachea expand. But this was yet another disappointment. We found the same damaged segment, narrow and flaccid. It looked inflamed and bled easily. The examination also revealed a mushroom-like polyp growing on the inside wall of the trachea. This had probably developed because of the irritation caused by the tube. The stricture, therefore, instead of improving with the attempt to stretch the trachea, had gotten even worse. How could we leave a tube in the trachea if it was also causing damage to the trachea?

The doctors were beginning to lose patience. Anne was going to be four years old. I remembered the article concerning the Canadian child, whose tube had been removed when he was three and a half years old. We had gone beyond that length of time and still had seen no apparent progress!

The Intensive Care doctors and Dr. Tristan began to consider surgery, something they had not been in favor of before. They consulted Dr. Niemand, a surgeon at Leclerc Hospital, who decided to hospitalize the coming August.

What could we do with our summer before that time? We thought of buying and equipping a trailer as a "mobile home hospital." We had just received an unexpected sum from my insurance company because of Anne's handicap. We decided to use it for this purchase, adding some of our savings to the insurance money. The idea was original and daring, but it helped us overcome the disappointing results of the latest bronchoscopy, as well as the fear caused by anticipating the upcoming major surgical procedure scheduled in August.

In June, we found the second-hand trailer we had been looking for. We parked it on "our" small Brittany island. Electricity came from a long electric cable plugged into the trailer; the medical equipment worked. The first evening, we relished the happiness of being together as a family in our little house on wheels, independent and far from the dust and various daily annoyances of urban life.

Month after month, we were learning to cope better with Anne's handicap. We no longer simply waited for an extubation. The Lord was giving us the grace of happiness, and allowing us to appreciate our daily life as a family.

From Hospital to Hospital

It was with both excitement and apprehension that Anne and I entered Leclerc hospital on August 12, 1985. The surgery unit was almost empty as it usually is during the summer vacation period. We were given a large room with two beds, and I was allowed to stay with Anne. There seemed to be almost no staff at all. I took care of Anne completely on my own and found this "self-service" system to be exactly what I wanted. The nurses seemed to be relieved by our independent system, and we saw almost no one, but all the necessary equipment was there: suction machine, catheters, humidifier.

Dr. Niemand first had to see the damage himself, by yet another bronchoscopy. He wanted to remove the polyp by laser. He invited me to observe as he operated. I had so far been present for only three of Anne's numerous bronchoscopies. This was the most spectacular I'd seen. I stood next to the table. After Anne was asleep, the surgeon first inserted the bronchoscope into her throat, then inserted the laser catheter into the bronchoscope. He then fired the laser in short bursts, as if he were using a machine gun. This made little noise, but a lot of smoke. It was quite frightening to see Anne lying on her back with her head thrown back, mouth open, looking like an erupting volcano!

I feared Dr. Niemand might be too aggressive and laser too far. I feared he might puncture Anne's trachea, which was already damaged and probably fragile. Instead, Dr. Niemand asked for a little more laser power. He burned into the mucus another few tenths of a millimeter. I prayed, "Lord, stop him before he goes too far!"

The procedure lasted 30 minutes. Dr. Niemand looked satisfied. He was confident he had destroyed the whole polyp and proposed not to reinsert the tube. He felt that the polyp had obstructed three-fourths of the airway and might have caused the previous failures. I was very skeptical. It did not seem wise to me to attempt to remove the tube at the end of a bronchoscopy, when, as we had seen before, it usually took Anne about a week to recover from this aggressive procedure. Dr. Niemand addressed my concern by remarking that Anne was now breathing well without her tube. I told him Anne initially did well in the minutes and even the hours following extubation, but would then worsen. He was nevertheless optimistic.

This seemed too easy. If a few minutes of laser were sufficient, why had we waited four years to do this? Did he realize we had already gone through multiple failures? Dr. Niemand was friendly, but obviously believed he had nothing to learn from me about Anne, since this was his area of specialty.

The nurses who took Anne, without her tube, into the recovery room rejoiced in advance about the success of the operation. They were surprised by my lack of enthusiasm. Refusing to speculate on the long term, I asked to sit with Anne in the recovery room, and obtained permission to do so.

Soon I witnessed the deterioration I had expected. Anne was progressively becoming short of breath. The surgeon had left, and I was alone with a child who was doing worse by the minute. An anesthesiologist came by every now and then and admitted that Anne was not doing well. I wished the surgeon would have come by. He who was so certain of his success and had been close to convincing me that he had actually removed the major cause of Anne's breathing difficulties!

After a few difficult hours, the level of deterioration was identical to that of the previous attempts. The anesthesiologist called an assistant of Dr. Niemand, who allowed me to reinsert her tube to the original depth. Immediately, I put my cheek close to the opening of the new tube and I felt the reassuring thread of air I knew so well. I suctioned the bloody secretions which had collected below the narrowing. Anne immediately improved. She was taken back to her room, where we had a good night's sleep.

The conclusion seemed obvious to me; despite removing the polyp, Anne was back where she was before the laser procedure. Where are we going, oh Lord?

The next day, I saw Dr. Niemand, who was surprised and disappointed by the failure, but of course less affected than I was. He talked about the possibility of a major surgery procedure, consisting of cutting out a segment of the trachea and then joining the two ends. The damaged zone would therefore be removed. The surgeon explained that this intervention would be very difficult for several reasons. The size of the resection was the first problem. The damaged zone was about two centimeters in a trachea that measured only six centimeters in length altogether. Secondly, Anne's ventilation during the surgery would be extremely tenuous. Finally, the position of the heart and major vessels on the right side rather than the left side represented complications for the surgeon, who would not be able to rely on usual anatomical points of reference.

Paul and I decided to contact Dr. Koop in the United States, for the second time. Until now, the extubation attempts although all ending in failure, had not represented major risks. Now, we had a new solution to consider, and, although very risky, it provided the hope we had been gradually losing over the months. The idea of healing Anne completely through a surgical intervention was appealing. We were facing quite a gamble. Our daughter's life was at stake. We had to ask for the advice of the best specialists and Dr. Koop would know them. According to my research in the University library, there were medical teams who specialized in surgery of the trachea in San Diego, San Francisco, and Toronto.

After waiting for several weeks with no reply, we lost hope of receiving help from the other side of the ocean. Dr. Koop surely had plenty of other things to do! His response finally arrived, and it was very specific. He had taken the time to write to several teams and was waiting for their replies. He invited us, first of all, to ask the advice of his friend, Dr. Verdun, in Marseille.

Marseille

We made an appointment with Dr. Verdun for December 23. We would take advantage of this trip to spend the Christmas holidays with my aunt Monique on the French Riviera, only an hour away from Marseille.

The Saint-Gilles team was not enthusiastic about our decision to consult a doctor in Marseille, but we were determined to obtain the opinion of this surgeon. Dr. Niemand felt the suggested surgery was too risky, and he seemed to be the only surgeon in Paris who could have undertaken this procedure.

In November, I passed the examination for the specialty in industrial medicine. I was encouraged, because I was among the 9% of candidates who had passed! This was the result of great effort. I wanted to meet the challenge of pursuing difficult studies even with a sick child at home. I was certainly satisfied with my accomplishment, but my powerlessness in the face of my daughter's handicap reminded me that my efforts would mean nothing if I relied on my own strength. I found this truth in the following verse:

"...What do you have that you did not receive? And if you did receive it, why do you boast as though you did not?" [2]

A page in the book of my life, which lasted two years, had turned. I had obtained my specialty diploma. What would I do now? As long as Anne was trached, I only considered working part time, and very close to home. It was therefore likely I could not practice industrial medicine for several years. Was I accumulating diplomas that I would never use? As I thought about this question, I was encouraged by reminding myself that God has a plan for all of this. Without Him, I would not have passed this selective exam, under such difficult conditions. It was only by His grace, His daily help, that I had succeeded. If God had supported me constantly so that I might be able to finish my studies, surely I would be able to use these additional skills later. I was no longer flying blind. I was caught in a bit of a fog, certainly, but I had a perfect Person in the control tower with whom I needed to stay in constant communication. He would show me the way in his time.

Dr. Verdun had already received Anne's complete file from me. We were absolutely startled by his first words: "We need to operate on this child as soon as possible. I would have done it a long time ago if I had seen her earlier," he said.

How had we missed such a simple solution in the past years? We had mixed feelings, vacillating between acceptance and doubt, about Dr. Verdun's strong opinions. Such a peremptory, quick opinion seemed suspect, especially since the Parisian doctors had been so circumspect. At the same time, we knew that Dr. Verdun was not just any doctor. He was world famous in his specialty, was the president of an elite medical society, and had been recommended to us by the Surgeon General of the United States. Were we in a position to be skeptical of his advice?

---

[2] I Corinthians 4:7.

Dr. Verdun insisted: "How can you have lived with a tracheotomized child for five years? Can't you see that her life would be transformed if she got rid of it? Do you know about the dangers of a prolonged tracheotomy? One day, you'll wake up and find her dead in her bed, asphyxiated by a mucous plug!"

He opened wounds we were struggling to heal. Of course we were afraid of mucous plugs! Of course, I got up every night to make sure Anne was still breathing. There had not been one morning in the past four years when I had not physically felt the fear of seeing her dead.

Dr. Verdun irritated me. If Anne had not been operated on before, it was for good reasons. Paul and I had not been waiting passively for four years until we could hear this man's opinion! At the same time, I wondered if he might be right.

We answered that we were not against a surgical solution, but for now the ENT doctors and Parisian Intensive Care physicians had advised us against it. Dr. Verdun explained that surgery belongs to surgeons, and that ICU doctors are often overly cautious and conservative. When we told him that Dr. Niemand, the surgeon at Leclerc, had found the operation too risky, Dr. Verdun replied that he would take care of the technical problems and would show us children who had undergone such an operation on the trachea. He was almost convincing!

Still skeptical, I told him about the difficulty presented by her unusual anatomy: "Anne doesn't have a right lung, and has a case of dextrocardia. Isn't that going to cause problems as far as the incision is concerned? He replied, I will enter through the sternum, as I usually do in tracheal surgeries."

He spoke as if he did these surgeries every day! I told him I would indeed like to meet children who had undergone such an operation. He set an appointment for a bronchoscopy and a tracheography. I did not want to exclude any options, but I was also determined to be in control of making the decisions. This would not be easy, considering Dr. Verdun's unfailing self-confidence. But we were not about to give him a blank check for Anne's life which others had spent months to save with such great difficulty!

We returned to my aunt's home on the Riviera. After an enjoyable week there, I took the train with Anne to Marseille, where we went for the appointment with Dr. Verdun on December 23.

We were given a room in the general surgery unit, where the atmosphere was very different from what we had known in the ICU. Most children were hospitalized for minor operations and walked around all day. I was struck by the lack of competent personnel. No nurse was present during the night, and only one nursing assistant was responsible for the entire unit. Many mothers took care of their own children. The children who were alone were not well-attended. A little girl who had an appendectomy the previous day threw up her evening meal. No one was there to clean her up and take care of her. The mothers of other children rose to the challenge. These conditions did not inspire much confidence! Of course, after a tracheal resection, Anne would not be hospitalized here, but rather in the post-surgical intensive care. Yet it would be the same surgical unit, the same unit chief.

Anne was to have a tracheogram in the radiology department. Relations with the radiologist who performed the tracheogram were very tense. I was absolutely determined not to leave Anne alone with him. He did not know her case, and much could be risked by making a mistake in the positioning of the tube. Besides, it was an examination that the Saint-Gilles team had not performed, believing it too dangerous for Anne. I had promised myself never to leave her in such situations.

The examination was to take place under general anesthesia, in the X-ray room. I entered with Anne, explaining unhesitatingly to the nurse that I had to stay with my daughter. Probably a bit intimidated by my assertiveness, she let me in.

It was much more difficult with the radiologist. When he asked me to leave, I told him, smiling, that I would stay. He told me he never permitted the presence of parents during examinations, especially in the case of general anesthesia. I answered that I was a doctor and I took medical care of my daughter on a regular basis.

"That's an even better reason for you to leave," he told me.

He seemed determined, but so was I. I told him that Anne had already had bad experiences in radiological examinations.

"Which brings me back to my point. Please leave," he said again.

Realizing that it was useless to argue further, I looked him straight in the eye, gathered all my courage and said, "I will not leave."

"In that case, he said as calmly as I had, I will not perform the examination."

I did not answer. Was he bluffing, or would he actually have Anne brought back to her room? Would he tell Dr. Verdun he had not been able to perform the examination? As for me, I preferred renouncing the tracheograms to leaving Anne in his hands without being present. I prayed God's will would be done. After all, perhaps it was preferable this risky examination not take place.

The radiologist went to the other side of the room. A few minutes later, an anesthesiologist began to put Anne to sleep with a mask. So the radiologist had given in! The doctor came back and, carefully avoiding my eyes and without a word to me, began his work. He injected a contrast medium into Anne's trachea through the tube, then removed the tube, and took X-rays. As I had expected, he did not measure the catheter exactly before removing it, and reinserted it to an inappropriate depth when he had finished. He went to the light board and commented on the X-rays in a hushed voice with his students, carefully avoiding to inform me of his impressions. This did not matter much to me. Dr. Verdun would tell me the results and I would soon be able to look at the X-rays for myself.

I put the tube back in its correct position and followed the orderly who brought Anne back to her room. The struggle was over.

At 8:00 am the next morning, Anne was taken to the operating room for bronchoscopy. However, Anne and I had to wait in the adjacent waiting room until noon. At noon, Anne was taken for the bronchoscopy. She was tired and tense. Half an hour later, I saw her again when she was taken back to her room by an orderly. She was not yet awake and was breathing with difficulty. The orderly waited quite a long time for an elevator, and I took advantage of the delay to check on her tube. It was two centimeters higher than its original position – well above the strictured zone! Had Dr. Verdun willfully attempted to slide the catheter to a higher position?

In that case, how could he leave Anne alone with an orderly, without medical supervision? Had he simply reinserted the tube without paying attention to its previous position? Anne had had dramatic respiratory arrests because of mistakes of a few millimeters, and Dr. Verdun was, inserting her tube more than two centimeters above its correct position! I was really aggravated. Was I going to put my daughter in the hands of this surgeon for a much more risky intervention? Did he think that a bronchoscopy was not important enough for him to proceed with the best care and caution? As for me, I would follow the biblical maxim:

> *"Whoever can be trusted with very little can also be trusted with much."* [3]

I watched closely over Anne and had a doctor called. An assistant of Dr. Verdun's arrived. I asked him if the tube had purposely been placed in this position. He answered vaguely and I was convinced the mistake was the result of a simple oversight. I told him that the tube had been placed above the narrow area of the trachea and asked him if I could reposition it correctly. I said all this in a submissive and amiable tone, but I was really delighted to put him in his place!

With his authorization, I pushed the tube down. The secretions then came abundantly and I was able to suction them. My decision was made; Anne would not be operated on here.

---

[3] Luke 16:10.

Before we left, I saw Dr. Verdun in his office. In a very academic tone, he gave me his impressions. I smiled inwardly. Despite his efforts, I was not impressed! His conclusion was the same as before. It was necessary to operate quickly. He succeeded in worrying me by telling me that the one lung had already been damaged and that this would worsen until the narrowed segment obstacle was removed. According to Dr. Verdun, most of the narrowing was on the main bronchus, not on the trachea itself. In his opinion, the tracheography showed a collapse of the main bronchus causing a distal dilation of the lung.

"This news is not very encouraging," I told him, worried.

"Don't be discouraged, we can intervene by transplanting some cartilage from the ribs or tibia on the trachea and main bronchus," he replied.

"How can you surmount the difficulty of ventilation during such a long and delicate procedure?" I enquired.

"I'll intervene using a heart-lung machine," he said.

"That's a high-risk technique!" I said.

"We've mastered it well. We practice it daily here," he retorted.

"I will discuss this with my husband, and, of course, with the medical team who followed Anne in Paris. This is a major decision," I replied.

"Of course. This is for you to decide. But don't wait too long, it is necessary to operate before she turns six," he emphasized.

"You know that we are in contact with your friend Dr. Koop, and we are also thinking of seeking the advice of specialists on the trachea in the USA," I said.

Would he be offended if we sought advice in America? We certainly did not want to distrust French doctors, who had saved Anne's life, but we also wanted to consider as many opportunities as we could to help her live a more normal life.

In fact, we had been considering, for the last few weeks, a year-long stay in the USA, which would allow us to have all the time we needed to consult one or several surgical teams, and possibly have Anne operated on. While there, Paul could take advantage a sabbatical year devoted to working on his doctoral thesis.

Upon our return to Paris, I told the Saint-Gilles doctors about the disappointment we experienced in Marseille. They seemed relieved. After looking at the tracheography, they were more reassuring than Dr. Verdun had been regarding the condition of the left bronchus as well as the lung.

At the same time, we received a message from Dr. Koop. He recommended Dr. Baker, a Toronto surgeon, who seemed the most competent and experienced doctor who could deal with Anne's case. The Saint-Gilles team knew Dr. Baker's publications and reputation and also thought very highly of him. Dr. Baker was known as a cautious and patient man. After having translated Anne's file into English and having sent it to Toronto, we received a response from Dr. Baker. He was willing to hospitalize Anne in order to assess whether or not an operation was appropriate.

Chapter 13
America

Toronto

Our family was finally set for our big trip to Canada and the United States. We left on June 15, after fond farewells to friends who did not hide their concern for us.

Dr. Houlette had designed a humidifier for us to use in the plane, Anne-Marie had prepared a set of catheters. Their help, at this time when Anne's destiny was no longer in their hands, touched me. Both of them symbolized for us a page of our story, and no one really knew what was ahead of us.

The dreaded transatlantic flight went well, and we did not need to resort to the oxygen. We simply had to instill normal saline into Anne's tube every half-hour, and percuss her during our layover in New York.

The arrival in Toronto was worrisome; we had to carry our humidifier, suctioning machine, a large bag with bottles of normal saline and trach tubes, not to mention the equipment for Paul's doctoral dissertation (microfiches, books and computer). At customs, we had to explain at length the nature of these suspicious-looking machines.

After an endless series of hallways, it was a joy to discover that a Canadian couple had come to welcome us! After chatting a bit, they took us to a small house provided by a Toronto church in the center of the city. A member of the church welcomed us there. She had filled the cupboards with food, her children had prepared a box with toys for Matthieu and Anne, and the beds were made. Toronto is a densely populated city and the rents are very high. It was generous of this church to provide us with a house, a vivid example of Christian solidarity.

At the hospital, Dr. Baker was very cautious. He decided to dilate the tracheal narrowing by inserting a different tube, in order to avoid, if possible, major surgery which he deemed extremely risky. For several weeks, Anne went through a long series of unsuccessful attempts. The first tube was too short, and Anne experienced respiratory distress as early as the following night. The second tube, longer but too thick, could not go into the narrowed area. Each attempt choked her. Dr. Baker ordered a third tube, and asked its designer to be present during the intervention in case last-minute changes proved necessary. When Dr. Baker tried to insert it, Anne, usually so cooperative, struggled to keep him from doing so. She might have remembered the choking she had suffered from the previous attempts. She had to be strapped onto the table. Three persons maintained her head and limbs in place. The ordeal had begun. It lasted more than an hour and was very stressful.

As soon as Dr. Baker inserted the tube, Anne stopped breathing. The radiologists tried to visualize the situation on the screen. Anne choked to the point that she began to lose consciousness. As she began to faint, and as I was holding her head, Anne looked at me with frightened eyes. How hard this was! I prayed, "Lord, help Anne, quickly!"

Dr. Baker did not understand. The tailor-made tube was of the same length as Anne's usual tube, yet the air did not pass through it. He removed it all. I suddenly had an idea and told him about it. Perhaps the difference was due to the bevel. Her usual tube was beveled on the bottom end, which allowed the opening to be directed towards the left main bronchus as well as maintaining its role as a tracheal stent. The surgeon decided that it was worth a try. The designer of the tube beveled and polished its cut end. Anne now had a few minutes of respite, as her other tube had been reinserted in order to allow her to breathe. I could not take her in my arms, since she was strapped onto the table, but I stroked her head and spoke softly to her.

Dr. Baker was a bit disillusioned, "If this doesn't work," he said, "I don't see what else can be done." I prayed silently while the catheter was being prepared. I did not feel capable of going through many more of these excruciating experiences, and I prayed for God's deliverance. Dr. Baker came back with the beveled tube. I was still praying and did not notice him. He gently patted me on the shoulder and his look was full of sympathy. "It's ready," he said.

Anne looked at me with panicked eyes. She cried out, "Mommy, Daddy, no more torture!" She fought the tube, which made it difficult to insert. But it went through and, miraculously, so did the air! We waited a few minutes. Anne was breathing well. They took X-rays, the tube was all the way down and the bevel was open toward the main bronchus. Dr. Baker was happy, now certain of his success.

We left the hospital without a dime. We had 52 Canadian dollars and 55 cents. We had to pay $50 for some medicine and $2.50 for parking, leaving us only 5 cents. Fortunately, the Lord had provided for everything. We had been invited o dinner by a Canadian family that evening. After dinner, Paul went to a church meeting with them. Upon his return, he told me the church had prayed for Anne and a board member had given him an envelope with $60 (just a little more than what he had payed at the hospital), even though we had not said a word about our financial concerns. Thank you Lord! Beyond the immediate help provided, this blessing assured us God was watching over us at every moment, and was taking care of all our needs.

Anne seemed to be doing well with her new tube, so a few days later we decided to visit some friends in Québec. After a few days on the road, her condition began to deteriorate. Anne, who very rarely complained, begged us to remove this new tube and reinsert the old one. As soon as we arrived at our friends' home, Anne suffered a complete respiratory arrest and lost consciousness. We were far from any hospital and had no oxygen.

There was only one hope. We had to change the tube immediately. We pulled the current tube out easily, but it proved very difficult to reinsert the original. The tracheal lining was irritated and infected. My hand began to tremble. I knew time was running out, "Lord, please!" The tube went in a little, I felt it enter the narrow area, and air went through feebly. Anne stopped convulsing and went to sleep. We had not seen much of Québec, but decided to go back to Toronto immediately.

We were all exhausted by these traumatic experiences, and Anne needed to recover from the ordeals. Paul and I decided to keep the original tube and leave for Oregon where we would spend the school year. As for Dr. Baker, he decided to orient his research toward a new technique, the use of a spiral which would be placed in the trachea in order to keep it open. He foresaw several months of research and experimentation on animals.

"I'll let you know," he told us, "when the time has come to try it on Anne."

Oregon

Four thousand kilometers later, we settled into our home in the "Far West." We anticipated many new experiences, as well as new friendships.

The principal of our children's school had her share of surprises; Matthieu and Anne did not speak English, and we were putting Anne in kindergarten despite her tracheotomy! The principal agreed to this, but asked me to attend the first few days with Anne to help both children and teacher adjust to a most exceptional situation.

By Christmastime, both children were at ease in their new language and Anne could do without me. I acquired a pager, and being able to be easily contacted, I benefited from greater freedom.

I went through times of discouragement, often missing my home country and my friends, but was certain at the same time that our presence here in this country was not by chance. God was watching over us. I became all the more dependent on Him since my familiar network of friends and responsibilities had been left behind. I did not know what the future held for us, but regardless, I wanted to tell the world that God is real and His presence makes all the difference. While the children were in school, I began a new project. I began to write about our experiences of the previous five years. I hoped to someday use this story to tell of God's faithfulness in our lives.

"I will praise you, O Lord, with all my heart; I will tell of all your wonders." [1]

The cold and rainy Oregon winter was not any easier than winter in Paris.

One day, I went out on foot to run an errand, leaving both children at home. I took the pager with me, so the children could call me if needed. As I was walking back, still about a mile away, I received a call. Worried, I looked for a telephone, without finding one. I did not know which direction to run to find a public phone. The device rang a second time, then a third, while I was running home.

I imagined the worst possible scenario. Matthieu was frantically trying to call me while Anne was having a respiratory arrest. Was I going to arrive too late? I saw a man washing a car in his driveway, and, breathless, told him my story in a few words, "Please, would you drive me home right now?" Taken aback and a bit suspicious, he agreed nevertheless, seeing my panic. Two minutes later, I rushed inside the house, full of anguish. Both children greeted me, smiling.

"There you are!" Matthieu said, "I called you to see if we could eat an apple, but you didn't answer, so we went ahead."

I collapsed on a chair, aware that my concerns as an adult were not the same as theirs, and so it should be.

Back to Canada

In June, we received an invitation from Dr. Baker to try his new spiral tube, and we returned to Canada. This small cylinder, which

---

[1] Psalm 9:1.

had embodied our hopes for a year, was covered by a plastic substance to which Anne was allergic.

Another failure to face. This time, Dr. Baker had no immediate new solution in mind: "Return home to France," he said, "and come back when Anne is ten years old. If we have no other solution, we will then consider major surgery on the trachea. The older the child is, the better her chance of success for that operation."

Another five years. Five years of reprieve for Anne who faced an apparently inevitable, but dangerous operation, with life and death at stake.

Chapter 14
Another Way
– May 1988

Following our family's year-long stay in Oregon, we returned home to France. Anne, now seven and a half, was finishing first grade with a tracheotomy. We had to face the thought that she would perhaps have to keep it her whole life. We had been back in France for ten months, and nothing, medically speaking, had been attempted during that time.

At Saint-Gilles, Drs. Houlette and Tristan had consulted each other and suggested attempting to insert a short tube. I was not very optimistic, as we had tried this, without success, several times in the past few years. Anne had never been able to go for more than six hours with a tube that did not entirely cover the flaccid segment of the trachea. The doctors advised me to try a new kind of tube, which would better follow the curvature of the trachea.

On Wednesday, May 11, I was ready to try the short tube at home. Spring had come and we would take advantage of the Ascension holiday to make several attempts, so Anne would not have to miss school. I brought home several tubes of varying sizes, and also made sure the oxygen tank was functioning well.

At 10:45 am, after having untied the lace holding the tube, I let Anne take it off herself. I did not want to make a big deal out of this. It was better for her to be relaxed about the event, even if it was the most significant one of the year for us. Matthieu cooperated by reading her a story while I inserted the short tube. She coughed a bit, then breathed well again, and completely forgot the change of tube, going back to her games.

Thirty minutes later, she began coughing. After an hour and a half, she was coughing constantly, and began to have trouble breathing. I replaced the tube with another, which was of the same length, but narrower, hoping that it would help limit the irritation. She continued to cough.

Paul joined us for lunch. We sat at the table, but neither Anne nor I could eat, Anne because of the coughing, and I because of the anxiety.

Anne started to complain: "Mommy, there's something stuck."

I immediately thought of the narrowed segment, which was probably forming an obstacle under the tube. Did this mean there had still been no progress? She was coughing incessantly now, and I could see bloody secretions. Things were going downhill and it was obvious the shorter tube was not sufficient. It had only been two and a half-hours that the flaccid area had not been covered!

At 1:00 in the afternoon, I gave up, after confirming the respiratory trouble with the stethoscope. I sadly brought the oxygen bottle and a long tube, and removed the short one. The hope I had clung to for a year was vanishing.

The radio was commenting on the results of the presidential elections. In France, the president is elected every seven years. France now had a new president, but after seven years Anne still had her tracheotomy.

Suddenly, I remembered an event from the Bible. It was as if Jesus were speaking directly to me:

> *"He replied: 'You of little faith, why are you so afraid?'*
> *Then he got up and rebuked the winds and the waves, and*
> *it was completely calm."* [1]

I was in this state of discouragement when a surprising thing happened. As soon as I removed the shorter tube, Anne declared that it

---

[1]   Matthew 8:26.

felt "much better" and began to eat. I decided to leave her alone a few minutes before inserting the long tube. Fifteen minutes later, she was no longer coughing and was breathing well.

Hanging on to this very slight and illogical hope, I decided to leave the tube out and see how long she could cope. I did not, however, want to leave the opening on her neck without the tube too long, fearing it might close over. I also knew that it was wishful thinking to believe that she could breathe without any tube at all, since she could not even hold on an hour and a half with a shorter one!

After lunch, Anne began to play with her dolls. I sat down close to her to sew, trying to conceal my anxiety, but constantly keeping an eye – or, rather, an ear – on her.

At two o'clock, her friend Janelle came over and, tired of playing with dolls, both girls decided to organize a roller-skating show for my benefit! I let them have fun, even though I feared physical exercise would worsen an already precarious respiratory condition.

Anne was breathing a bit loudly, but did not seem to be bothered at all. At 4:30 pm, she was still doing well, despite the roller-skating demonstration. I called Dr. Houlette at Saint-Gilles and told him about the failure of the short tube, and the very clear improvement without a tube at all. Perplexed, he told me that he had not anticipated this scenario! We agreed that I would wait for the evening, then reinsert the tube when Anne went to bed (if she continued to do well). We did not want to prolong leaving the tube out through the night, fearing the trach opening might close over.

The following day I repeated the process. The most important thing was to teach Anne to cough productively. We could not suction her since the tube was no longer there. As she grew tired of having to cough and spit every hour, wanting rather to play, we invented games, such as the person who coughed the loudest would win. Our respiratory therapy was more efficient that day. That evening, she was doing well and I had no difficulty reinserting the tube. Her opening had closed only a little during those twelve hours. Even better, her secretions were no longer profuse when I reinserted the tube. All of this was surprisingly encouraging! However, Paul and I refrained from rejoicing too soon, and we were succeeding quite well. We had experienced so many failures that such a simple victory – a miracle – did not seem likely.

The next day, May 13, I decided to send Anne to school without her tube. I accompanied her and explained to Anne's teacher, who became somewhat anxious. At 10:00 am, I went to the playground to have Anne cough and to assure myself that everything was all right. The teacher told me about the astonished looks on the children's faces when Anne began to read without her tube. As the air leaked through the tracheal opening, she had a completely different voice, not as well controlled as with the tube blocked by her chin. Everyone had stared at Anne and she became very embarrassed. The teacher had then explained the difference to the children and the incident was rapidly forgotten.

I continued to keep Dr. Houlette abreast of Anne's condition. He advised a bronchoscopy before attempting a longer or even permanent extubation. I preferred to avoid the bronchoscopy and continue these attempts at home, but I had to accept the logic of his advice. I scheduled an appointment for June 2.

I used the two intervening weeks to try Anne at night without the tube. I would have to observe Anne all night long, something I could not easily do without help. Paul, overloaded with work at the end of the school year, definitely needed to sleep. Our only solution was to have electronic surveillance via the monitor. I decided to ask the advice of Saint-Gilles hospital.

I took Anne there one day after having removed her tube in the morning. This was the first time I had taken her there without her tube. Everyone marveled at her wonderful appearance, her pretty dress and her lace socks, but no doctor, no nurse dared give any opinion on her respiratory condition. Dr. Houlette listened to her chest and said nothing. The stakes were so high, the result so uncertain! The ICU loaned me a monitor, permitting me to proceed.

On May 18, I was ready to attempt this nighttime trial. Anne was nervously excited, very interested in the monitor. I had to wait until she fell asleep before plugging it in, otherwise she would watch the electronic oscillation as if it were TV! I brought a mattress near her bed, simultaneously praying and watching the screen. Everything seemed normal; Anne was sleeping peacefully and breathing noiselessly. I fell asleep awhile. At 2:00 am, the upper alarm of the machine rang, then stopped functioning. Anne was doing well, but I could no longer count on that machine to monitor her.

At 6:00 am, Anne was still breathing quietly. I joined Paul who was getting up and told him Anne's apparent success through the night, but also of my fear to find Anne plugged up upon awakening.

At 7:30 am, I awoke her. It was a school day and I wanted to integrate this extubation into a life as normal as possible. She got up as though nothing had changed and came to breakfast. She had forgotten that she no longer had a tube! The most extraordinary thing to me was that she made no noise while breathing, whereas during our previous attempts, the secretions accumulated as the hours passed. Surprisingly, nighttime went better than the daytime.

I tried to restrain my enthusiasm in front of the children, but right away I called Paul at work. Victory now seemed within reach. Anne was doing very well and did not want me to reinsert the tube for the school day. I also felt an overwhelming desire to leave her extubated.

"But this was not wise," I thought. "We must not take the risk that the tracheal opening could close before being sure, by means of the bronchoscopy, that she had a good chance of success." After seven years of waiting, we could certainly wait a few more days. We savored these days of hope, with only a vague fear they would lead to another disappointment.

I thus put the tube back in place and Anne left intubated for school. The teacher was somewhat bewildered. Sometimes Anne came breathing through a tube, sometimes without the tube. Anne explained to her, "Now we take the tube out at night, but we put it back during the day to keep the hole!"

At that time I was reading *Victory over Everest*, the tremendous feat of Edmund P. Hillary. I felt I was experiencing the same trial of patience and a similar relentless struggle toward victory. Caring for Anne was the work of an entire team for many years, but, like the ascension of Everest, only a few of us were completing the journey to the summit, to taste the thrill of victory.

Many friends had borne burdens with us, in practical ways and in prayer, these past seven years. We experienced setbacks, accidents, moments of discouragement, and sometimes were tempted to give up; but now we were approaching our goal. We could not let down our guard or ease up on our prayers. Like the mountain climbers bivouacking in high altitude close to the summit, we were also patiently waiting for the best conditions to make the final charge to the top.

Chapter 15

Final Charge To The Top

N o one, except Dr. Houlette, knew that we were intermittently removing Anne's tube. Still fearing failure, Paul and I minimized the importance of the event in our own eyes. We also desired to keep our victory private for a short while.

The following week was busy with preparing for the bronchoscopy. Anne and I went to the hospital for the preparatory tests: blood work, anesthesiology consultation, and X-rays. All this preparation was long and complicated and I had great difficulty once again putting up with the "system," which was robbing us of some of the joy of Anne's victory.

On June 2, we had an appointment at 7:45 am for the bronchoscopy. As I feared, we had to wait hours until 1:00 pm. Anne had to fast and saw no benefit in waiting an entire morning on a bed. I had an irresistible desire to return home and forget about the whole thing. Would the anesthesiologists and surgeons, always in such a hurry, appreciate having to wait five hours for no apparent reason? Would they wait at the bedside of their child such a long time?

At 1:00 pm. an orderly came for Anne. I was surprised to see her back twenty minutes later. When the surgeon finally passed through the room, he explained briefly but clearly, with diagrams, the current state of Anne's trachea. Large mucous folds still obstructed half of her airway over a length of three centimeters but left enough space for air to pass. An extubation could be attempted if accompanied by good respiratory therapy to help Anne expel the secretions stagnating between these large mucous folds. This confirmed our clinical impressions. I was encouraged, even if the state of Anne's trachea was far from normal.

I went to the ICU and related the results of the bronchoscopy to Dr. Houlette. We agreed to attempt a permanent extubation on June 7, at home, then to hospitalize Anne in Intensive Care for the night of the 8th and 9th, the critical time when the stoma risked closing. Dr. Houlette himself would be on call that night. With the trial of the bronchoscopy finished, Anne and I went home where she awakened.

Three days before the anticipated day of Anne's extubation, two young women traveling from abroad called to announce their arrival on the following day. I would certainly not have chosen the extubation date to have guests. I realized, however, that their arrival could help reduce our tension as this exciting time approached. I still worried the extubation would fail!

The evening of the extubation, we had fun with the two girls. We sang, played music and a board game. At 10:00 pm, our two guests retired to their room. The time to extubate Anne permanently had now come. I had waited for this moment nearly seven years! I had decided not to make a big affair out of this, but the four of us felt the importance of that moment.

Anne asked us to take a picture of her with the tube before removing it. We had no film, and I told her it would be more interesting to take pictures without the tube, for we already had hundreds of them with it! I wanted us to experience the exaltation of the moment together, for we had all lived with the consequences of this tube for seven years. Anne and I joined Paul in Matthieu's bedroom, where I removed the tube. Removing the tube was such a simple gesture and one already performed so often. Then we prayed together, asking the Lord to help us live the following days by faith.

Anne had trouble going to sleep. Even though she didn't talk about it, she was a bit enervated by the event. Lying down next to her, I took my Bible and read God's promises in the book of the prophet Isaiah,

*"So do not fear, for I am with you; do not be dismayed,
for I am your God. I will strengthen you and help you; I
will uphold you with my righteous right hand."* [1]

This victory would be both God's and ours; I should not worry,
rather rest in His power.

The night went well, as we had hoped and expected. The next day
was a first. Anne was now extubated for more than twelve hours. We
expected the closing of the tracheal opening, thus hindering an easy
reintubation. This period of time would be critical.

I was nervous. The hours were not passing quickly enough for my
liking. Anne had to go into the ICU for observation that evening.
What could we do while waiting? This June day was cold and rainy
and I dreaded letting Anne play outside. We decided to go to the
movies in Paris, near the hospital. Anne would thus be calm and
indoors.

We consulted the cinema programs. We had to leave right away in
order not to miss the beginning of the film *E.T. the Extra-
Terrestrial.* Suddenly, Anne was nowhere to be found! We searched
the house in vain for her. Everyone was a bit upset, almost forgetting
that the main reason for going to Paris was not the movie!

We finally found Anne with a neighbor lady who was showing her
how to feed a baby blackbird. Apologizing to the neighbor, we sped
off toward Paris. At the cinema, Anne, sitting next to me, was breathing in a noisy fashion similar to that of E.T. I was less and less sure
that Anne was going to succeed. I kept a sterile tracheal tube in my
purse, ready to act if she suddenly deteriorated.

Once in the ICU, Anne was taken to a patient room. It seemed
strange to leave her here, although this was the plan. The tracheal
opening was not yet completely closed. I really wanted Anne at
home. Dr. Houlette, however, was flatly opposed. It was better Anne

---

[1] Isaiah 41:10.

stayed the night in the ICU, for her opening would likely close in the coming hours.

Paul and Matthieu returned home via subway, and I stayed with Anne. As she was doing well, we received permission to leave the hospital and eat in a neighboring cafe. It was a very special time for both of us. After we ate, I left her at the hospital for the night, but I was not without anxiety.

I awoke at 5:00 am. Was Anne reintubated? At 6:15 am, unable to resist any longer, I called the ICU. The nurse told us Anne was sleeping quietly and there had been no need to do anything during the night. I was reassured temporarily but still dreaded the moment when she would awaken. This was the time when respiratory accidents had often taken place in the past.

At 8:00 am, I spoke with Dr. Houlette by phone. He was completely confident and told me there was really no reason to keep her another day. Now I was the one who was skeptical and he was the confident one!

When I arrived at the hospital in the late morning, Anne was not in the ICU, but was drawing pictures in the computer office. She was breathing better than the previous evening and I was finally reassured. Anne-Marie had taught her how to do her own respiratory therapy and she gave me a rather successful demonstration.

We waited for Dr. Tristan to come and give his opinion. He thought Anne was doing quite well and was visibly very happy. He had been one of the first, six years earlier, to advise us to be cautious and patient. I thanked him warmly for his good counsel, he muttered a humble response, but I saw in his face great satisfaction to have made the right choice.

Victorious Ascension: The Eiffel Tower!

We were free to leave! This time, it was the victorious discharge we had longed for! No one dared say it or even think it, but we all felt this way. Anne was leaving without her tube.

I was tired and the nervous tension had given me an awful headache. I was anxious to leave for home before the evening traffic jams. Anne, however, had another idea. I had promised her "someday" we would go to the top of the Eiffel Tower as Matthieu had often done with his father. I knew, indeed, that the day for this ascension had arrived. This was only the second time I had visited the Eiffel Tower. The first time was the day I met Paul, and, now 16 years later, the day of Anne's successful extubation. The Tower thus became a historical monument for our family!

We were perspiring in the humidity of the elevators, which were crammed with tourists, but nothing could spoil our joy. I wanted to declare in every language to these people from all over the world that they were experiencing an historical event, a great victory! I contented myself with smiling at everyone. I must have given the impression I was really excited about this ascent! For me, without being conscious of it then, going to the top of the Eiffel Tower symbolized another climb, longer, riskier and finally successful today. Our daughter was breathing by herself!

We saw Paris from on high, while a whole new world awaited us below; a world of living without a handicap!

Relapse

I believed in victory now! Four days after the extubation, I called a few friends to give them the news. I had hesitated to make this news public, fearing it was too soon to declare victory!

On the evening of the fourth day a sudden aggravation put everything into question. At about 5:00 pm I noticed that Anne was no longer outside playing with her girl friend. I called to her in her room. No answer. I went there and found her lying on a couch, pale and complaining of a stomach ache. She was breathing well and I thought that she had eaten too many sweets during her snack at the neighbor's.

I brought her into the living room where I could watch her. She started vomiting, but had no fever. Her breathing became rapid and noisy. I wondered if the vomiting was digestive, or signaled the onset of a respiratory infection, which would be much worse.

Unfortunately in a few hours' time, the latter hypothesis was confirmed. Thirty minutes later, Anne's temperature climbed to 101.3° and, a half-hour afterward, went above 102°. In two hours, her secretions changed from a clear liquid to thick, greenish-colored muck. Because of the speed of the deterioration, I feared a lung infection which, in a child with one lung and a tracheal malformation, could be fatal.

I immediately administered antibiotics that Anne just as quickly vomited. I called my friend Corinne, a neighborhood physician, who came to support me until midnight. She was a real comfort. I called the ICU and they told me to bring Anne in if her condition worried me too much. I only wanted to do this as a last resort.

In the early morning, Anne, who had slept very restlessly, was experiencing tachycardia and shortness of breath. Helpless, I watched her condition worsen each hour. Without a tube I could not suction out the infected secretions stagnating in her windpipe. I prepared the necessary material to reinsert a small tube via the tracheal opening, which was only half-closed. I also verified the proper functioning of the oxygen tank.

I was still hopeful. Even if I had to reinsert the tube, Anne had held on for four days and we would try again. I was aware that God knew Anne better than anyone did and that He would protect her once again. I thanked Him for taking care of her like a caring father. Perhaps this episode was only a minor setback. After all, the extubation had been almost too easy. We had prepared ourselves for a fight and had encountered no resistance. Now as the difficulties began I felt at ease, as if trials were old acquaintances.

We needed a bacteriological sample and a chest X-ray as soon as possible. I took Anne, pale and short of breath, to Saint-Gilles. A vigorous session of respiratory physiotherapy relieved her somewhat but she remained very listless until noon, vomiting any food and even water that we gave her to drink. The bacteriological exam revealed a streptococcus. The X-ray showed an infected area of her lung. We waited for the effect of the antibiotics Anne was now receiving intravenously.

At about 2:00 pm, Anne improved just as spectacularly as she had deteriorated. Anne's breathing became slower and more regular. She wanted to get up and eat. She was no longer vomiting. At 5:00 pm she was doing gymnastics at the foot of her bed. Could she win this battle without reintubation?

I spoke to the ICU physician. He told me that, in his mind, he never considered reintubating her. According to him, this episode had proved that Anne was capable of surmounting a respiratory infection without being suctioned through a tube. That same evening, I brought Anne back home. The entire episode had lasted only 24 hours.

Summer vacation arrived. Anne had now been without her tube for 20 days. The opening was still half-open and would probably have to be closed with a few sutures. Should it be done before our vacation?

Anne had always linked the prospect of the tube's removal with the possibility of learning to swim. The summer of her seventh birthday was before us, her first summer without a tracheal tube. Should we close the opening and consider her healed? It was tempting! Drs. Houlette and Tristan advised us to leave the orifice open. It was our lifeline in case of a major setback in her condition, since we could reinsert the small tube in an emergency.

We were disappointed. Once again, this summer, Anne could not play in the water like the other children. Disillusioned, I declared to Dr. Houlette: "In the last analysis, there is not much difference with her life when intubated. She needs to be given respiratory therapy, and she can't even go swimming."

"Don't say that!" Dr. Houlette reproached me gently.

I immediately regretted my words. Anne's extubation, successful for 20 days, without major surgical intervention, was indeed a miracle. Was I to allow myself to become discouraged by a problem related to swimming? Anne could breathe by herself. Caution had always been the right choice and now was not the time to give in to a whim.

Faithful to our adventurous spirit, we took a long trip by trailer to Austria and Yugoslavia, less than one month after the extubation. We took along antibiotics, several tracheal tubes of varying caliber, and the suction machine "just in case"! Protecting the opening with a plastic adhesive film, Anne was able to take advantage of a few careful swims.

During the first eight months following the removal of the tube, Anne had to constantly take antibiotics, in order to avoid a pulmonary infection. We continued daily respiratory therapy and the opening remained covered by a gauze pad.

Other than this minor care, Anne lived an absolutely normal life. Unable to join swimming lessons, as she would have liked, she became part of a gymnastics club. She went to school very regularly and had absolutely no schooling to make up.

In February, we took a week of vacation in Switzerland and Anne learned the joys of snow and skiing. How we appreciated not having to transport all our medical equipment! We only took antibiotics, gauze pads and a small trach tube that we hoped to never have to reinsert.

The tracheal opening was sutured closed, ten months after her extubation, in April 1989.

Chapter 16
Safely Into Port
– Victory

It was now June 1989. Until now, we had not dared celebrate Anne's victory. Our ICU physician friends would never have allowed themselves to assure us Anne was out of danger. We currently had an entire year behind us without a trach tube and it was legitimate to be very optimistic.

Since January, Anne had become gradually less easily congested. She required less frequent respiratory therapy sessions, finally not needing them at all. Beginning in February, we progressively ceased the antibiotic treatment without seeing Anne become infected immediately afterward.

It is probable the tracheal mucous membranes, previously irritated by the constant presence of the tube, were slowly healing. Eight months had been necessary for the mucosa to return to normal, and for the vibrating hair cells to function once again in order to expel the secretions naturally, as they do for everyone. We are not even conscious of this marvel.

In May 1989, one month after the closure of her trach opening, Paul and I noticed that for the first time we were living without any medical assistance – no apparatus, no medicine, no special care. At

Anne in grade school, age eight.

age eight and one half, for the first time, Anne was healed. The chronic respiratory insufficiency we had feared had not taken place after the extubation. With her heart to the right, a single lung and a trachea still malformed, Anne lived a perfectly normal life. It was a dream come true.

The moment had arrived to open the champagne, an event which the chief of the Saint-Gilles ICU, Dr. Péron, had awaited since 1982.

On June 14, we went to the ICU to celebrate Anne's recovery with those who had worked with us. It was a wonderful victory celebration. Seven years had passed since Anne had left the ICU in 1982, and most of the doctors and nurses had changed wards or departments. We thought there would be few left we would recognize. We were astounded to see almost all the "alumni." Anne-Marie, the ICU Head Nurse, our friend whose help had been so precious in the most critical moments, had invited the entire team there. We had the immense pleasure of seeing Dr. Maurice once again. He had made a special trip from the hospital in suburban Paris, where he was now department chief, to meet a healthy eight year-old girl, whom he had saved when she was only four months old. We had not seen him for seven years.

Dr. Tristan, the ENT specialist who was always so busy and yet there at the right time, came as well. Claude and her two children came from the village where she lived with her husband Pierre, a General Practitioner. Maria Sebti made a special trip from Casablanca with Chakib! The dream of reuniting our two children when they were well came true that day. Dr. Péron was photographed with the two children on his lap. He was happy to celebrate these two great victories of his team.

Finally, Anne-Marie and Dr. Houlette, who represented for us the continuity and the security of the ICU, were there. A few nurses and nurses' aids had also come for the occasion. An entire medical team, whose calling was to save the lives of children who would not have otherwise lived, celebrated with us that day. It was a very moving time. The champagne flowed, and Anne-Marie concluded with these simple words, "What a beautiful story!"

I close this narrative of the great adventure that God allowed us to experience. We would not have chosen it, but we don't regret it.

Like the disciples of Jesus, tossed to and fro by winds of an angry sea, we had survived a dangerous time, with Jesus' help. We risked shipwreck if we took our eyes away from the One who guided us.

Like the apostle Peter trying to walk on the water, we were sometimes tempted to accomplish the extraordinary in exceptional circumstances. Like him, we were panic-stricken as soon as we looked at the circumstances that threatened us, rather than to Jesus who is the Master of circumstances. Like Peter, we then began to sink, until, returning to the basics, we realized our weakness and cried out to God, "Lord, save me!" Jesus never failed to hold out His hand and say to us,

"...You of little faith," he said, "why did you doubt?" [1]

Are not all the tempests of our lives like this, whether it be illness, grief or divorce? When we climb into the boat with him, he accompanies us and the storm is calmed. The power of faith surpasses the most cruel trials. We must learn to follow step by step and with humility the One who created us, without remaining passive in the midst of difficulty. We must learn how to steer the helm, be vigilant, and ready to sail ahead when God gives us the necessary strength.

"Some sailed over the ocean in ships, earning their
living on the seas.
They saw what the Lord can do, his wonderful acts on
the seas.
He commanded, and a mighty wind began to blow and
stirred up the waves.
The ships were lifted high in the air and plunged down
into the depths.
In such danger the sailors lost their courage;
They stumbled and staggered like drunks – all their skill
was useless.

---

[1] Matthew 14:31.

Then in their trouble they called to the Lord, and he
saved them from their distress.
He calmed the raging storm, and the waves became
quiet.
They were glad because of the calm, and he brought
them safe to the port they wanted.
They must thank the Lord for his constant love, for the
wonderful things he did for them.
They must proclaim his greatness in the assembly of the
people,
And praise him before the council of the leaders." [2]

Life Lessons

At the end, how had we grown through this trial? I will speak for myself, even though others, and principally Paul, Matthieu and Anne, were also beneficiaries of "life lessons." I am still learning these lessons. I don't pretend to have arrived at a stage of advanced wisdom. I am still surprised and disappointed by my failings, and my relapses in areas I thought I had mastered. I have been strengthened but am not unshakable! The Lord still has work to do in me!

All these years, I insisted on maintaining my responsibility toward Anne, who, even at the hospital, was mine. I realized that I needed to grow in self-confidence and also become more amiable with the personnel caring for Anne. Being too timid results in poor communication. It was absolutely necessary to avoid this danger and attempt to engage in light personal relationships with the caregivers. I began relationships with comments on the weather or working hours, keeping myself from criticizing or even agreeing with criticism from any medical employee toward the hospital. Having established a personal relationship, Anne was no longer an anonymous case. The hospital, in spite of its weaknesses, represented for us a progression toward greater knowledge, even if it did not result in

---

[2] Psalm 107:23-31. Today's English Version.

Anne's immediate improvement. The hospital is also the only place where it is normal to have a handicap and we felt reassured in this setting. When I return to the hospital with Anne, she and I are happy. Anne does not see these visits as painful experiences, in spite of what she had gone through there.

On a deeper level I discovered, like Job of the Bible, my smallness before the Creator of the world. I realized that I had no control over the life and death of those that I love. I can only put my confidence in Him who loves my family with a more perfect love. I received a great lesson in humility:

> "...I will walk humbly all my years because of this anguish of my soul." [3]

I had to admit my children do not belong to me. A mother suffers greatly if her child is taken away from her. Do we really have rights over our children or are they rather a privilege to cherish?

I learned to manage my anxiety as well as possible, without guilt. I realized that fear is a normal reaction which must, like sadness, be freely expressed, sometimes even physically. The knot in the stomach, lack of appetite, and tears are all normal and acceptable expressions. On the other hand, to be controlled by chronic anxiety can lead to the deterioration of our inner being. In a way, anxiety is to be included in the trials of which the apostle Paul speaks:

> "Every test that you have experienced is the kind that normally comes to people. But God keeps his promise, and he will not allow you to be tested beyond our power to remain firm; at the time you are put to the test, he will give you the strength to endure it, and so provide you with a way out." [4]

One of the greatest benefits I received during this trial was a better understanding of God's grace. His grace is a present, an unmer-

---

[3]   Isaiah 38:15.

[4]   I Corinthians 10:13. Today's English Version.

ited gift, always available to me. In case of an emergency, it is comparable to the help of an emergency rescue ambulance. God gave me grace as I called on Him by faith, that is, with the confidence that He would act.

God's grace was addressed to me personally and directly by God Himself when I needed it. My friends also participated in this grace when they helped me to bear my burden.

Grace is experienced in the present. Grace comes neither before nor after the need. It cannot be stocked up in advance. When the Israelites wandered in the desert, God sent them miraculous, heavenly food, called manna. This food allowed them to stay alive one day at a time. In spite of their desire to stock up for the following day, they could not do so – the food spoiled immediately. In this way, God showed His people how to live by faith, that is, by counting on Him one day at a time. In the same way, we cannot stock up God's grace (help):

> *"The Lord's unfailing love and mercy still continue, fresh*
> *as the morning, as sure as the sunrise."* [5]

Grace is not conditional, for we do not have to meet certain conditions to obtain it. We must only accept it. This is why many refuse God's salvation offered by grace alone. It seems too easy and our pride makes this extremely difficult to accept!

We cannot demand God's grace, nor give Him orders concerning our wants. "God, heal my daughter, she must be home for Christmas!" is not how we should talk to God. He alone knows the best moment and the best way to act. It is He who measures the time necessary for fashioning us according to His plan.

---

[5]   Lamentations 3:22-23. Today's English Version.

"Be glad about this, even though it may now be necessary for you to be sad for a while because of the many kinds of trials you suffer. Their purpose is to prove that our faith is genuine. Even gold, which can be destroyed, is tested by fire; and so your faith, which is much more precious than gold, must also be tested, so that it may endure." [6]

God also taught me the value of love. I discovered that love is the most precious thing in our existence:

"Meanwhile these three remain: faith, hope and love; and the greatest of these is love." [7]

Love is our fuel. Without love, our life will break down. I recognized the value of married love, faithful and constant in adversity. Love is often put to rude testing by life. Husband and wife are two strands only held together by a third strand forming the braid – God Himself. No married couple is strong enough intrinsically to be sure they will not break apart in adverse circumstances, trials or unexpected temptation. Only God, who ties us together, can give us this strength. We must remain united to Him to keep our love alive and vibrant.

I learned to appreciate the value of parental love. My love for Anne took me without hesitation or regret to the hospital 270 days in a row. It is this love that led Paul to prefer puppet shows with Matthieu to professional advancement. What would remain for us, if we were to lose the love of our children?

In addition, I grasped the value of deep friendship. A human person is more important than the object, relational values have to take priority over accomplishments or activism. I had been somewhat distant in my relationships with people, oriented toward my own success. God is still working to help me be less selfish, more understanding, and better able to listen to others. This process will never be completed in this life, but this trial helped me take a big step

---

[6] I Peter 1:6-7. Today's English Version.
[7] I Corinthians 13:13. Today's English Version.

forward. I learned to give and receive at the same time; to give without counting, without asking anything in return and to love the beloved person for who she is, not only for what she does. Thank you Maria, Claude, Anne-Marie, and Elisabeth, for being friends with me, for teaching me the value of friendship. Thanks to this trial, I began to open my life to others. I am more vulnerable, but life is much richer!

Epilogue

Anne – June 2002

It was 13 years ago that my tracheotomy tube was removed. I will be 21 this summer, a senior at Gordon College near Boston, majoring in history. I play the cello and enjoy working with our college's homeless ministry in the Boston inner city.

I still have the tracheotomy scar. Every time I see the scar in the mirror, it reminds me of God's faithfulness .When I was in grade school, I was ashamed of this mark for it set me apart from the other children. I was afraid of being rejected and tried to hide it as much as possible. I came to personal faith in Christ at age 12 and gradually came to appreciate the positive testimony of this scar to others and to myself.

When asked about it, I share my story: In His grace, God saved me twice, from physical death and from spiritual death. He has proven his faithfulness to me in so many ways.

Anne – May 2002.

Agnès:

Just a few months after Anne's extubation, I found employment in industrial medicine and was able to practice my medical speciality for several years in various industrial companies in the Paris area. This part-time position allowed me to remain available for the needs of my family. In addition, my experience with Anne allowed me to empathize with my patients in the workplace.

In 1991, when Anne was 10, she was admitted for a few hours to Saint-Gilles hospital to receive oxygen for a bad case of bronchitis. We were given a brief glimpse of the past and were reminded what was at stake, for since her extubation, Anne had been living a very normal life.

We also realized we needed to close the previous chapter of our lives and go on to new horizons. We opened our hearts and minds to a very special people who had suffered greatly during our own decade of trial: the people of Lebanon.

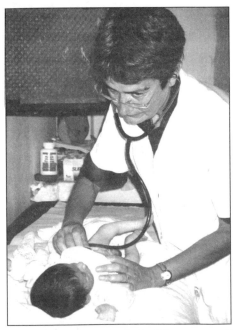

Baby Lucile was born in September, 1991 in Beirut and came to our home in February 1992. Her adoption was a marvelous family project that became reality. This new little sister from Lebanon revealed an amazing power to heal the tensions and fears of our older children. She also became our direct link to Lebanon. After several short-term trips to Beirut, our family moved to the land of the Cedars in 1996. This was also a return to Paul's family roots. His mother's parents, driven by poverty, had emi-

Agnès examining baby in "shantytown" dispensary, Beirut – 2002.

grated to the USA at the beginning of the 20th century. God does things in such creative and unexpected ways, even over generations.

At age 14, Anne underwent plastic surgery to repair her tracheotomy scar. I had grown fond of this scar, a witness and reminder of God's great power in our lives. But Anne's life was ahead of her and we did not need to dwell on the past. Though her scar is gone, I want to continue to build on the lessons learned during these difficult years:

> *"Forgetting what is behind and straining toward what is ahead, I press on toward the goal to win the prize for which God has called me heavenward in Christ Jesus."* [1]

After having completed high school in Beirut, Anne, age 20, is now a senior at Gordon College, near Boston, studying History and Spanish. Allowing her to go 6000 miles from home was surprisingly easy for me. Perhaps even more than other parents, I knew that God was in control of her future. Since beginning her studies in Boston, she has also lived several months in Spain and in Italy.

Matthieu studied one year at the Lebanese American University in Beirut, then graduated from Wheaton College near Chicago in 2000. He accomplished a one-year political internship at the German parliament in Berlin and is now completing a Master's program at the Institute of Political Studies in Paris.

It has been a great joy to see a deep friendship develop between Matthieu and Anne over the years. Although our family now lives on three different continents, we communicate regularly by e-mail and feel that we are a close family.

After 15 years of ministry at the Nogent Bible Institute near Paris, Paul was called to become Academic Dean of the Arab Baptist Theological Seminary in Beirut. This institution trains Arab believers from the Middle East and North Africa in the Arabic language for a

---

[1] Philippians 3:14.

wide variety of ministries in the region. He is also involved in leadership positions in Middle Eastern and European theological education.

In 1993, I began a compassion ministry with Catherine, a Swiss missionary teacher, in the shantytown of Hayy Al Gharbeh. This camp is located in the southern Beirut suburbs destroyed by the 16-year Lebanese war. God opened my eyes to a whole new world, the world of the most deprived – poor, sick, abandoned mothers with young children – refugees. These people face injustice daily and do not have the means to speak out, to defend themselves. I had felt so helpless during Anne's illness. I could now better understand those who cannot help themselves.

Our life in Lebanon has been a new adventure for us, so different from our life in the eighties in France, yet clearly lying in the continuity of God's will for our lives.

In 1996, we opened literacy classes for the unschooled shantytown children. In 2000, we opened a free dispensary where several hundred families come regularly for primary health care. We call our work "Tahaddi" in Arabic, meaning "challenge." Each day we encounter great challenges, feel overwhelmed at times, yet we must remember again and again to return to God for new strength.

We count it a privilege to fight this world's injustices and to rely on God's great power. I dedicate this book to the children of the shantytown. It was Anne's story that led me to them.

Agnès and Anne – 2002.

Paul:

I have been both a spectator and an actor in Anne's story. I witnessed God's daily, tailor-made grace to our family, and had the privilege of assisting Agnès in the battle for Anne's life. Naturally, this story is written from Agnès' mind and heart, from her perspective. My role was more behind the scenes, sometimes intensely engaged, at other times I was more like a cheerleader on the sidelines. This trial interwove Agnès life and mine together even more strongly. In a sense, knowing that as it says in Ecclesiastes "a cord of three-strands is not easily broken," in this story, Agnès and I became one strand, God was the second, and the trial itself was the third, binding us together with Him and with one another.

As I look back over this period of 20 years, several things come clearly into focus: God used this trial to deepen and strengthen my overall life, ministry and perspective. I am still benefiting from this investment and believe that I always will.

These events were also a special gift, giving me a special relationship with each of my older children, forged in the crucible of suffering. I was rudely awakened from my "workaholism" and need to succeed to relate to my offspring at the deepest level. What a privilege!

The story of Anne led us clearly to the adventure of Lucile's adoption and our subsequent move to Lebanon. Once again, God showed His creativity in revealing His will. The precious gift of our beautiful Arab daughter is an incredible treasure.

Last, but not least, I have become conscious that every breath is a gift, not a right. As I continue to struggle and grow with new challenges, I realize what a privilege it is to know God personally and to count on His presence, while I have breath and beyond.

We often say, "We wouldn't have chosen it, but we don't regret it." 20 years later, I believe that with all my heart.